The Ongoing Journey

Awakening Spiritual Life in At-Risk Youth

Also from the Boys Town Press

Books

Common Sense Parenting

Common Sense Parenting Trainer's Kit

Helping Teens Unmask Sexual Con Games

The SAY Book: A Program for Sexually Abused Youth

The Ongoing Journey: Awakening Spiritual Life in At-Risk Youth

Sexually Abused Children in Foster Care

What Makes Boys Town So Special

I Think of My Homelessness

Boys Town: A Photographic History

Teaching Social Skills to Youth

Working with Aggressive Youth

Preventing Suicides of Youth

Effective Skills for Child-Care Workers

Caring for Youth in Shelters

Videos

Helping Your Child Succeed

Teaching Responsible Behavior

Videos for Parents Series

Sign With Me: A Family Sign Language Curriculum

For a free Boys Town Press catalog, call **1-800-BT BOOKS.**

The Ongoing Journey

Awakening Spiritual Life in At-Risk Youth

Edited and
published by

BOYS
TOWN
PRESS

BOYS TOWN, NEBRASKA

#32238086

The Ongoing Journey

Awakening Spiritual Life in At-Risk Youth

Published by The Boys Town Press
Father Flanagan's Boys' Home
Boys Town, Nebraska 68010

Publisher's Cataloging in Publication

(Prepared by Quality Books Inc.)

The Ongoing journey : awakening spiritual life in at-risk youth / edited by the Boys Town Press.
    p. cm.
    Includes bibliographical references and index.
    ISBN 0-938510-48-7

    1. Youth – United States – Religious life. 2. Socially handicapped youth – United States – Religious life. 3. Church work with youth – United States. I. Boys Town Press.

BV4531.2.O54 1994   261.8'3423
                                         QBI94-1521

CONTENTS

From Theory to Practice

Book Credits

Editing: Terry Hyland
Ron Herron

Cover Design: Rick Schuster

Page Layout: Michael Bourg

INTRODUCTION

The Ongoing Journey

THOMAS J. EVERSON

*W*elcome to *The Ongoing Journey*, a collection of essays exploring the spiritual and moral life of at-risk young people. These essays, gleaned from four symposiums conducted at Boys Town, Nebraska, between 1989 and 1993, and supported by a grant from the Lilly Endowment, represent perspectives from some of the most outstanding professionals in research and practice in the field of youth work in the United States. Since they are edited versions of the contributors' oral symposium presentations, an effort has been made to retain the conversational, narrative flavor of the original presentation in each essay.

The first section of *The Ongoing Journey* is entitled "Essentials of the Journey." This section contains four essays which set the stage for delving into the implications of cultural sensitivity and pastoral practice shared through the articles in the sections, "Multicultural Perspectives" and "From Theory to Practice." These articles serve to frame our journey within an understanding of what influences the spiritual and moral life of at-risk youth, and of how this essential knowledge forms the way we seek to serve young people.

Essentials for the Journey

DR. ROBERT COLES begins our journey with two essays: *The Profile of Spirituality of At-Risk Youth* and *Some Thoughts on*

1

Religious and Spiritual Education with Vulnerable Youth. Dr. Coles's insights, stories, and wisdom, accumulated during a lifetime of exploring the spiritual and moral life of young people, serve as a fitting starting point.

The REVEREND CHARLES SHELTON'S essay, *Mental Health and Conscience Functioning in At-Risk Youth*, provides a framework for understanding and facilitating conscience formation in young people.

DR. DAVID ELKIND, in an essay entitled *Facilitating Spiritual Growth Among At-Risk Youth*, challenges youth workers to foster spiritual growth among the young people they work with in congregational, synagogue, and parish settings.

Multicultural Perspectives

The four essays in this section seek to expand our horizons as we explore the implications and richness of four cultural experiences that affect spiritual development in young people. These cultural focuses include Hispanic/Latino, African American, Asian American, and Native American perspectives.

SISTER VERONICA MENDEZ, RCD, opens this leg of our journey with her essay, *Sometimes Even God Needs Help.* Sister Veronica introduces us to the Hispanic/Latino culture, a culture deeply bound up in a relationship with God that does indeed affect every facet of personal and family life.

DR. NSENGA WARFIELD-COPPOCK'S essay, *Approaches to Resiliency: An African-Centered Perspective,* enriches our understanding of an African American experience of spirituality deeply rooted in and affected by the ritual that is indigenous to the culture. She offers examples of rituals and proverbs that provide insight into how we might guide African American young people, as well as youth of other cultures, along their spiritual journeys.

The REVEREND DONALD NG introduces us to the Asian American culture in his essay, *Portrait of Asian American Youth: Cultural Issues for Ministry*. The Rev. Ng begins by focusing on common prejudices and perceptions of Asian Americans within American culture. Building upon the strengths of the Asian American culture, he challenges youth workers with 10 appropriate responses that can be integrated into the ministry with Asian American young people.

The REVEREND REAVES NAHWOOKS offers *A Native American Perspective* to our travel supplies for the journey. The Rev. Nahwooks provides a rich foundation for understanding the Native American culture, contrasting the importance of its spiritual life with the consumer orientation of American culture today.

From Theory to Practice

DR. LORRAINE MONROE moves us into the home stretch of our journey with her essay, *Effective Strategies for Working with At-Risk Youth*. Dr. Monroe draws from her own personal experiences of serving youth in educational environments to offer practical advice for all youth workers.

The REVEREND BRUCE WALL expands the scope of possibilities for the practitioner in his essay, *Setting At-Risk Youth Free Through Spiritual Growth*. The Rev. Wall's personal narrative of his own journey from adolescent faith to an adult faith that he has employed to reach teens on the street offers further concrete strategies for affecting the spiritual lives of inner-city youth.

The REVEREND BUSTER SOARIES defines and challenges each of us to put into practice the basic ingredients for evangelizing at-risk young people in his essay, *Characteristics of Conversion*. Filled with anecdotes and insights gleaned from years of frontline experience with young people, the Rev. Soaries offers practical strategies for the spiritual conversion of youth.

The final essay, by THOMAS J. EVERSON, is entitled *From Risk to Resiliency: Faith Skills for the Journey*. This essay articulates a practical skills-based approach for fostering moral development within the lives of at-risk youth. The insights offered represent the best of current thinking and practice developed from the years of work devoted to nurturing the moral life of at-risk youth at Father Flanagan's Boys' Home.

So sit back, soak in, reflect on, and flesh out these thoughts as you ponder the road you are traveling with young people who are in search of their spiritual lives. We hope the works of these child-care professionals can give you new ideas, renew your commitment, and inspire you to continue to touch the lives of youth.

Essentials for the Journey

CHAPTER ONE

The Profile of Spirituality of At-Risk Youth

DR. ROBERT COLES

I'd like to start with my own struggles, which go back to the beginning of the work I do. I was originally trained in pediatrics and the first work I did with children took place at the very time we had a polio epidemic in Boston. It was probably the last polio epidemic this country will ever see. It was in the mid-Fifties and Massachusetts General Hospital and the Children's Hospital were both filled with young people and older people who were paralyzed — their arms, or their legs, or even the breathing center of the brain, so they couldn't breathe without being put in iron lungs.

The Salk vaccine would come into common use about a year or two later. Meanwhile, here were all of these people, many of them children, who were paralyzed and facing the possibility, even the likelihood, of death. And I went about my medical work with them, doing whatever could be done to sustain them and edge them toward rehabilitative work with people who would teach them how to compensate for their loss due to the polio virus.

And yet in the midst of that work, I could not help but hear from these children all kinds of questions that were not directed to me as a physician. Maybe they weren't directed to me at all. They were directed ultimately, to what? They were directed to God, to nature, to fate, to circumstance, to chance, to luck. They were asking themselves Job's questions: Why did this happen to me? What did I ever do to deserve this? And what does this life mean anyway? If this is the outcome, I haven't even started and I'm through.

On and on these remarks went. And the more I heard them, the more I began to realize that in the midst of a medical crisis, I was hearing moral and spiritual inquiry of a kind that can only connect with a long tradition that goes back again to Job, to the saints and sinners of all time. Namely to all of us. Especially to all of us when we are in jeopardy or pain and vulnerable, and begin to wonder who we are, what we are, and what this life means, if anything.

Now I also did some work with some children who had leukemia then. We're talking about the late Fifties, and we're talking about a time in medical history when there was no cure at all for leukemia. The only thing we had then was blood to prolong life a bit. No chemotherapy and none of the various medical maneuvers that now can cure 70 to 80 percent of the children with leukemia.

And I well remember a girl I had gotten to know who was dying of leukemia. One day, she asked me whether I had ever been to the Red Sea. I looked at her a bit wide-eyed and said, "No, have you?" And she said, "Yes." So I said, "You've been to the Middle East?" She said, "No." I said, "Well, how could you get to see the Red Sea if you didn't go to Israel or to some part of the Middle East?" She said, "I have seen the Red Sea."

And then I thought, "Ahhhh, this young lady is troubled. This young lady is troubled and I'd better find out what the trouble is."

So I said, "What do you mean, you've been to the Red Sea?" Now, if I asked you, "What do you mean, you've been to London?", and you've been to London, you'd be insulted. But she was patient with me. She said, "I've been there."

She knew I was interested in children's drawings and she had done a number of drawings for me. (I was collecting drawings even then. I was interested in how they helped me communicate with children and, of course, most importantly, how they helped children communicate with me.) And she said, "I'll draw you a picture of the Red Sea."

I scurried around and got some crayons and paper, and the next thing I knew she was drawing a picture of the Red Sea for me. She started out with a red crayon and was going to put it to the paper. Then she put it aside without touching the paper and picked up a blue crayon. She started drawing blue and I realized this was the ocean or the sea. She looked at the red crayon as if she was tempted to use it but put it aside. But she continued with more blue on the upper part of the paper and then I realized this was the sky. Then she picked up a black crayon and she colored under the sky and the next thing I knew, there were clouds. Then she put a sun in the sky radiating but not getting through the clouds. Next, she picked up a brown crayon and started drawing circles and I began to realize she was putting an island in the midst of this ocean. Then she got some green and started drawing some trees and flowers and bushes, sort of like *Gilligan's Island* on television. She got a yellow crayon and put it down, and instead picked up an orange crayon and drew a human form. Then she picked up that red crayon again and coated the blue of the sea with red. And I thought to myself, "Aha, the Red Sea." The body was on top of this red, and then she did one more thing with a black crayon. She drew an arrow pointing from the body toward the island.

Then she said, "Here it is." I said, "What's this?" She said, "This is the Red Sea."

And then I pointed to the island. I said, "What's that?"

"That's an island," she said.

"Well, what's going on there?" I asked. She pointed to the human form and said, "If I get there, then I'll be better."

And then she looked at me and she said, "I don't know if I'm going to get there."

I said, "That body, that's you then." And she said, "Yes."

So I said, "I still don't understand you when you tell me that you've been to the Red Sea and yet have never left this country."

She didn't say another word. She just used her arm and she pointed. I can still see that arm pointing, the finger pointing, and my eyes following the direction of the finger and the next thing I knew, my eyes were focused on a bottle of blood on an IV stand.

And she looked at my face and must have decided that I was not quite ready for her interpretive skills. She thought I needed a little help. So she said to me, "That's the Red Sea." She had been, of course, immersed in a sea of blood that had sustained her, kept her afloat, as in that picture, but she knew that it was unlikely she'd really get through this ordeal to the safety of that island.

This was an experience that I've held in my mind, heart, and soul now for more than 30 years. She was a very important teacher, as many of our patients are for us. A very patient and tolerant teacher. Patients often have patience, particularly with those who think they know a lot. She had shown a lot of patience with me and had given me a lesson about her experience.

Interestingly enough, this was a biblically connected story, which I did not then explore with her — the whole question of the Red Sea — because I wasn't trained to, nor did I think it appropriate. But what I learned from her was her willingness to speculate and wonder, to ask questions of herself, to maybe even try to get me involved in this kind of introspection.

The next work I did connects directly with where I am right now. I worked as a consultant — they called me a psychiatric consultant — for the Lancaster Industrial School in Massachusetts. This is when I started taking training in child psychiatry.

The Lancaster Industrial School no longer exists — the name is a phrase out of the earlier days of American work and concern for children. It was a school that housed hundreds and hundreds of women who had gotten into trouble with the law. "Juvenile delinquents" they were called then. They were very tough people to work with. What I was asked to do more than anything was to prescribe medications even then to calm them down. But I also would sit with some of them and listen to them talk about their lives. (I also worked with delinquent boys who were under a program in Boston called the Citizenship Training Group [CTG].)

I remember the supervisor I had then, a child psychoanalyst who was working with such youth and also with alcoholics. I remember his willingness to surrender at times as he contemplated the troubles of some of these people who were not like the well-to-do, well-educated, and Alice Anns he saw four and five times a week on Marlboro Street in Boston.

Once, he said to me, "The problems here are severe and people like you and me do not always have the where-with-all to respond to them." And when he used that word "where-with-all," I thought he was signaling to me that he thought I needed more education and more knowledge, more psychiatric and psychoanalytic skills.

So I got into a discussion with him about that and I remember him very clearly telling me that the issues were not necessarily those of insight. The issues were those referred to by Erik Erikson when he wrote a book, *Insight and Responsibility.* The issues are those of conscience, of respect for one's self, of some kind of purpose in life that transcends psychodynamics. Purpose in life, he said, would transcend psychodynamics. This is not exactly how I was trained to think then, or I suspect, I would still be trained to think in the conventional psychiatric mold, which emphasizes the understanding of human motives and behavior but is not necessarily interested in those lives or purposes in life.

In any event, I learned what Alcoholics Anonymous could do for those alcoholics who visited the Alcoholism Clinic at Massachusetts General Hospital. And I learned how hard it was to work with so-called delinquent youth, who challenged any and all authority and who did not have psychological knowledge in mind as any great redemptive purpose in life.

Soon enough I was drafted into the Air Force and charged with a psychiatric hospital in Biloxi, Mississippi. In the Air Force, some of the corpsmen we used to see were 18 or 19 years old. They had gotten in trouble at home. They were hurt and vulnerable in various ways. And they got in trouble in the Air Force and ended up in our ward. A lot of them had broken all sorts of rules — were drinking too much, violating this or that regulation, had been in fights. They had problems with authority and were sent to us.

We were to either do something magically with them and get them better, meaning that they would comply and get on with the

Air Force and do their work, or get them out administratively. A lot of my work for two years was administrative — getting them out — after making a decision that whatever these difficulties were, we as psychiatrists in that military unit were not going to have much luck with them. After all, I couldn't take them on in analysis or intensive psychotherapy. The gun was held to our temples as well as theirs. Action was required, and quick action. And I was only in there for two years under the old doctor's draft anyway.

So that was more work with what we would call at-risk youth. They were maybe a little older than the youth who live at Boys Town, but not all that much. Many of them had life histories not unlike the young people who come to an institution such as Boys Town. Many of them had no parents. Many of them had been in trouble at home and in school and in the neighborhood for a long time. They had come into the Air Force in a hope against hope — theirs and the hope of their families, teachers, whatever — that they would shape up and reform. The Air Force as a reform school — another historical phase.

And we struggled as doctors to try and help this process on and oftentimes failed. What we were offering these young men was psychological knowledge, any and all that we had at our fingertips. And somehow that did not work. Many of them were insolent and fresh with us, even though we were officers, and wanted to know about our own lives and why we were in the Air Force. They also asked whether we'd ever felt like breaking rules.

To challenge medical authority that way, especially at that time, in the late Fifties and early Sixties, was itself an example of where these kids were. And I found sometimes, gradually after doing this work for some months, that I had the most success with those youth with whom I allowed myself to be more candid. Instead of, as a captain, telling them to shape up and stop turning the tables on me, I would occasionally say, "Look, I never wanted to come into this place. And if I could get out tomorrow, I'd leave. I was drafted, as all doctors were. And if I could get myself out with you, this would be a great day for both of us."

This kind of conversation opened up the door between me and them. A bit of friendliness and sharing my own difficulties with them, I began to notice, meant something to them and began to mean something to me.

Meanwhile, I got distracted by my struggles with school desegregation as I happened to witness it in New Orleans. By a total fluke, I was on my way to a medical conference during the riots and the mobs that plagued the little children who went into the desegregated schools in 1960 in that old cosmopolitan port city.

Ruby Bridges became a heroine of mine. She was a six-year-old girl who, in order to get into the first grade at France Elementary School, fought her way through a mob of about a thousand people who were telling her they were going to kill her. It was no fun for her when she did get into the school because then it was totally boycotted for the entire school year by the white population. So just picture a six-year-old girl in a totally abandoned school with a mob outside greeting her when she arrived and a mob outside greeting her when she left.

When I tell the story of Ruby Bridges, the climactic moment in the storytelling is my learning one day from her schoolteacher that this little girl had created a major ruckus on the streets of New Orleans by stopping one morning in front of that mob that persisted in heckling her during the entire school year. She apparently talked to the mob for about a minute. The mob didn't hear what she was saying but it surged toward her. And the federal marshals who were protecting her had to pull their guns out to stop this mob from hurting this child.

Later I would discover that this little girl had said a prayer in front of that mob. The reason she said that prayer that morning is because she had forgotten to say a prayer earlier for that mob. And I found out that she had been praying for this mob for months — praying for a mob that wanted to kill her. I found out what that prayer was. Several times a day, she would pray: "Please, please, God, try to forgive those people because they don't know what they're doing."

13

This from a girl whose life was in danger. This from a girl whose parents did not know how to read and write, and had no education. We would call them illiterate and be exactly correct. This from a girl whose life was in danger, yet could find forgiveness for those who endangered her life.

How does one understand this psychiatrically? How does one understand the family? No education; we say education is so important. No psychological support; they were threatened at home as well and the father lost his job.

Talk about at-risk young people. This was a family at risk. Utterly at risk. Socially at risk. Racially at risk. Educationally at risk. Culturally at risk. Economically at risk. You name the variable or the adjective, they possessed it.

And with all that risk, they were not going for — how is it put these days — counseling. They were not members of a support group, or any group. Well, that's not true. They were members of a group, if you want to call it a group. They went to church on Sundays. And they went to church and they stayed there for a long time, as my wife and I discovered when we went with them. This was not an air-conditioned church. And this wasn't a church you could get out of in an hour, looking at your watch, hoping that the hour would soon enough end. This was a church that went on and on. This was a church that could be described as a hard-praying church. Witnessing. Testifying. Exclaiming. Exhorting.

Once I turned to my wife and said, "Let's get out of here." I was sweating and tired. She said, "If you can walk out of this church, good luck." So we stayed and we listened. And after a while, we began to learn something about what was sustaining the Bridges family. It was a community of believers, utterly connected to the Old Testament and the New Testament, to the stories of the Hebrew prophets, to the stories that Christ told and lived out.

Ruby knew them. She knew the names Isaiah and Jeremiah. She knew the stories Jesus told. And she could connect those stories to her own life and did, in her praying life, in her family life, and in her school life, until she got through this.

Sometimes when I'd tell of her, people would turn to me and say, "Well, she must have been helped enormously by you," as if the only way that Ruby could have gotten through this was by seeing an American child psychiatrist. Talk about the patronization of people. The fact is that Ruby meant much more, I suspect, to me, ultimately, than I did to her. What meant most to her was the meaning she already had that she brought to this experience long before she had ever met me — the capacity to pray, a family capacity, and the capacity to even forgive. Forgiveness is not exactly high on the lexicon of contemporary psychiatry.

I got to know her. I got to know other children like her in various southern cities. I got to witness the civil rights movement. And over and over again, what I saw, I began to realize, was not only the psychological life that I'd been trained to study but also a moral life. Indeed, a spiritual life in action. Not only in thought but in action.

Because when Ruby would say, "Please, God, try to forgive those people," she knew whereof she spoke. And she explained to me: "You know when Jesus was in trouble, there was a big mob there. And they were ready to hurt Him. And that's what He said. And I try to say the same thing."

And, of course, skeptically, I pushed her and said, "Well, Ruby, do you always believe that?"

She said, "No, I don't always believe that, but I try to."

"How do you try to?" I asked. She said, "I close my eyes and I think of what it must have been like for Him."

Now this is a six-year-old child showing a capacity to connect in a fundamental way with earlier human experience, as we have been told of it. And she had learned this in a family that had taken no instruction in contemporary psychology or psychodynamics, and had taken no instruction in counseling and was not supported self-consciously by others in what we call a group setting. It had all taken place within the natural rhythms of a vulnerable people who didn't have to be told they were at risk. They knew damn well that they were at risk. And they had figured out over the generations what one does in the face of such evil. (They knew to call it "evil.")

In the face of such evil, a person calls upon a prophetic tradition, a tradition with its sources of understanding and even compassion for those who failed to understand one. This they knew in their bones. This they knew how to call upon. And they did.

I left the South. I went north and ultimately connected with the two people in my field of child psychoanalysis who made the most sense to me. One was Erik Erikson, with whom I taught. I taught as a section man in his course. And the other was Anna Freud, who really founded child psychoanalysis in London many years ago.

For years, I tried to gain from them a kind of understanding that would help me, in turn, to understand Ruby. Or, that girl with leukemia I'd met in the Children's Hospital. Or, for that matter, some of the so-called delinquent youth I'd met who showed a capacity to, as my father would put it, "shape up in their eyes." I wanted to find out what it is that enables such people to persist against great odds.

I will never forget a conversation I had with Anna Freud. Actually, it was one of the last conversations I had with her before she died in 1982. She was looking back over a long life of work with children. She was in her early eighties then. Her life of working with children had begun 60 years earlier. She started out as a schoolteacher and went on to become her own kind of child analyst, probably the first the world ever had.

And she said, sharing with me hard-earned wisdom, "I have spent my life trying to understand children. I think I know"—talk about a modest understatement—"something about how their minds work. But I must tell you, things have changed in this world."

And then she went back to the old Viennese days. She said, "You know, when we first started this work and August Aichhorn and I worked with these youngsters, there was plenty of trouble that we learned about in their lives. But one thing we could take for granted, and that is the conscience. Many of those children were frightened and anxious and difficult in so many different ways. But the common denominator of what they possessed was a conscience which, in turn, was wreaking havoc on them. They were the victims of a family life that was overbearing, inconsiderate, demanding, and hurtful in certain ways. But they also were part of a family life connected to a moral life. And that moral life, as strenuous as it was, was nevertheless at work in them."

(She was referring to her work with August Aichhorn, author of *Wayward Youth*, probably the first important book in which a psychoanalyst works with what we would call "troubled" or "delinquent" or "at-risk" youth.)

And Anna continued: "Over the years, I have noticed in my adult patients — never mind the children I have seen — less and less strength in the conscience. A conscience weakened by perhaps a society that is at work weakening all conscience. Firm standards undercut. The shifting sands of what is right and wrong."

And so she is switching into psychoanalytic theory. She said, "Strong instincts, clever adaptive egos, but no super ego or conscience with the strength or the muscle to deal with all of this. In contrast, the young people in the old days had tyrannical consciences, which indeed we had to work with to loosen up a bit and undercut a bit, but at least they had a conscience."

"The hardest thing in the world," she said, "is to offer a conscience or to try to help someone build up a conscience, when it's just not there."

She was addressing the issue of immorality and maybe what Christopher Lasch's book, *The Culture of Narcissism*, addresses — that it is possible these days for all too many of us to become so preoccupied with the self almost as an icon that there is no judgment of the self. I don't mean persecution of the self. But judgment of the self.

We are living in a society of psychology. People like Anna Freud and Erik Erikson and others who write books become secular icons of sorts. It's not a very enviable fate in the long run because one realizes that this is idolatry. And that what comes will soon enough go away. You know how these books come and go, and how the experts come and go.

17

Ruby's family called upon no experts. No newspaper experts peddling psychology. No textbook experts. No television experts. Their expert was a received religious and spiritual tradition that they had somehow managed to connect to their own personal lives. This is not so easy to do these days, for parents and for those of us who work with children in schools and in clinics.

Some of the best people who worked with the delinquent kids I used to "treat" were people who knew how to take these kids very seriously but who also knew how to take very little from them in the way of conning. Some were nurses and ward people who could speak up to the kids, who could exhort them, and could sometimes really tell them off.

Now I was not trained to tell children off. I was trained to understand children. And that's what people like me offer — understanding. I'm not saying that it's not a good thing to offer understanding to people. But what if there are people who are not ready to take understanding in the ways I'm trained to offer it? Those very nice, polite conversations based on a mutual understanding of what understanding is. The value of the teacher and the student. The value of the speaker and the listener. The kind of self-respect that some of us have received that enables us to be teachers or psychologists or psychiatrists or whatever we've become.

What if I'm talking with someone of radical skepticism based on radical injury? Someone consumed by righteousness of a certain kind — namely, rage that the world has treated him or her this way. How does one arrive at a common ground there? It's not an easy question to answer.

Let me move from that question to a bit of an answer I got one day. I asked Anna Freud to read Malcolm X's autobiography. Now there's an unlikely juxtaposition. When I handed it to her (we had become friends by then), she immediately said, "I've learned to be very suspicious of you with your books."

I said, "Well, this is a book that I think you'll find interesting."

"Why do you think that I will find this interesting?" she asked.

By time I had learned to deal with her and her parrying

questions. This is a form of tennis. And I lobbed the ball right back to her. I said, "Well, when you've finished reading this, maybe you can tell me why you think I thought it would be so interesting for you." (I later told my wife I said that. She said, "That is an insolent comment." I said, "No more insolent than the question.")

But Anna and I did it in good fun. She had a bit of a smile on her face when she asked her question and I think, with a smile, I was showing her how the expression goes that "it takes two to tango." And in a way I was dancing with her as we danced in this dreary field that I occupy, through the endless throwing back of the question (you know that trick I think, very well, from people like me), "How do you feel? I hear where you're coming from." And on and on that stuff goes.

After she'd read the book, she had abandoned these ploys. She said, "This is something to think about. What do you think really made that difference in his life?"

"I don't know," I said. "I thought you might help me with that."

She said, "I don't believe you. You do know. You had something in mind when you gave me this book in the first place to read."

And I then leveled with her. I said, "This is a fascinating story for me. Here is a story of a man who is a con artist, a jailbird. Let's call him at risk. And something happened to him. And he was not taken on in treatment. He did not sit in a support group or any other kind of group."

I'm not against any of this. But you can tell by my tone that I am somewhat skeptical of the way all of this has become used by us as we think about others. And overused. Used and overused.

What happened to Malcolm X is that he became a convert. In fact, he became twice a convert. He was converted by the Muslims and his behavior changed. And then toward the end of his life, he broke with the Muslims in certain ways and became converted to another view of the Christian message, and, indeed, of the Islamic message. Another world view. Another kind of spirituality.

I don't think he's alone. I think, again and again, people like

19

him, under that kind of apparent hopeless shadow have found within themselves that kind of ability to respond to a spiritual, religious community. And, if you want to translate that into psychodynamics, okay. But I think that psychodynamics ought to be put aside as we think about what it is that people need and can find. And what we all need and can find, and need to find and hope to find — including the therapists of this world — is some meaning in this life. That is our rock-bottom nature.

Our rock-bottom nature, I would argue, is not psychological. It is ultimately spiritual in this sense. We are the creature of language who through language tries to find answers to the rock-bottom questions of human existence: Where do we come from? What are we? Where are we going?

Psychoanalyst, Ivy League professor, big-shot expert in this or that subject, or extremely troubled kid at Boys Town or in the streets of New York or Los Angeles, roaming and running, rage-filled — we're all together this way. We have bodies. We have consciousness. We know that those bodies will soon enough disappear. And with them, consciousness. And we use language — a God-given attribute, a nature-given attribute, however one wants to describe it, but an attribute that enables us to look around and wonder. And we do.

As you read the books of philosophy or psychiatry or psychoanalysis, or psychology, or religion and theology, you will find in them, ultimately, the fundamental energy that you will find in a child at Boys Town or any of the other institutions you can go and visit where such children and young people reside. This energy is fundamentally moral and spiritual in nature. And it addresses all the questions that we address when we stop and are given pause by life: Hey, what does this life mean?

That's what I heard from those polio kids. That's what Tolstoy's Ivan Ilyich asks as he's dying. This is what you hear on any ward in any hospital, whether the people are utterly well-adjusted and affluent and psychoanalyzed, or as poor and as in jeopardy as you can imagine, socially, economically, culturally, educationally, racially, or whatever: "I am sick. I may soon no longer be, at least in the sense of my humanity on this planet." So we take pause, and we ruminate and speculate, and rage, and try to figure out, and are frustrated. But that is our fundamental human nature — to wonder about the meaning of life and to try to figure it out. And by no means to be always satisfied so doing.

That is the essence of spirituality for me. It is not necessarily attendance at a church or a synagogue or a mosque. And it can be embraced by someone who is profoundly skeptical about what is handed down by the religions as truth. But it entails a willingness and a capacity to wonder about things and to try to figure them out in an important way.

And this kind of spirituality, I would argue, is present in all of us in some way. The man headed for death in the electric chair. The person sick in a hospital. The person who is in some way stricken by life. And who has immunity from this? The answer, obviously, is no one.

And it is around that, I think, that we can begin to share our lives with one another at institutions like Boys Town. By the way, we ought to do so at some of the fancy institutions where so-called professors teach so-called privileged students. It's the same matter.

Who was this? Locke or Hobbs or Lincoln or Einstein or Gandhi or Newton or Darwin? What kind of human beings? What were they seeking? Answers to what? They too were fine-eyed human beings trying to know and understand, driven as you and I are by all the doubts of our humanity. In that sense, all intellectuality is an offshoot — you could call it a fancy word, a sublimation — of our humanity. It's that capacity to seek and try to understand that defines us and makes us different from other creatures on this planet. Not necessarily better, but different. If you want to get into the morality of various creatures, just think about how forgiving and loyal a dog can be in contrast to us.

I have not noticed at the Boston Psychoanalytic Institute a capacity for forgiveness and sustained attentive charity, even after 30 years of analysis in some of our more lengthy analyzed training of analysts, that matches what my dog, just like that, can mobilize all the time. Charity, loving kindness, loyalty, and the ability to transcend the petty foibles of these others called "human beings."

I don't think psychoanalysis in its most Messianic and utopian moments has ever thought that we, even with the most successful outcome of a therapeutic course of treatment, would ever get any of our patients up to the level of the ordinary household dog. So we have to live with ourselves. We have to live with ourselves, and the evil we will find in at-risk children is the evil that we must know in the mirror. It's the evil that has to do with our nature, our drivenness, if you want to get into psychoanalytic thought. It's what Saint Augustine knew long before Freud was born. Even Saint Augustine knew that the only way ultimately to come to terms with this is by the candid look inward, the honorable effort to understand one's self.

And we can link arms this way. Not just teachers and students and children who are at risk, but all of us who are at risk and vulnerable in our various ways. I'm at risk later this morning when I get on an airplane. I'm at risk in the sense that one of my coronary vessels could suddenly close up and that's the end of me. I'm at risk in the sense that I can be irritable, impatient, moody. And on and on these risks go. And until that is put on the table so that we link arms that way, then I'm afraid that we're not going to get too far with one another.

Now I have been to some institutions recently and I've met some young people, and they are called at-risk children. Some of them have been institutions connected to religious institutions and some of them have been secular institutions run by this or that person. And what does one make of these visits?

Well, what have I seen? I've seen what you all know is to be seen. I've seen people struggling with one another. The children and the young people are there and I've seen older people like us struggling with them and also us struggling with ourselves. That is, struggling with one another. I've heard a lot of psychology used. Boy, have I heard a lot of psychology used! As my wife would say, an earful of psychology. Which, of course, is the result of a mouthful of psychology being spoken.

I have encountered the irony that in religiously supported institutions, even institutions named after revered religious figures, psychology rules. In fact, psychology is not only summoned; it is believed.

The language of psychology and psychiatry and psychoanalysis is all in a kind of pastiche that is offered. I'm not here to throw an entire bucket of cold water on this — only half a bucket. But it can be ironic at times, hearing that psychology summoned as if it will give answers to these fundamental matters.

Young people ask again and again about matters that we ought to address. Namely, "What does this life mean and how could my life have come to this? And how does one look at all of this world in view of such experience?" Those are moral questions, if not spiritual ones.

Responsibility and insight without some larger view of meaning, I fear, is not quite as effective as some of us want to believe. When insight becomes effective truly, it is, I suspect, because it is capitalized. And the people who find it effective are believing in psychology with a kind of passion and conviction that is probably familiar to churchgoers or synagogue-goers. And I suppose I want to be understanding of that, too. Although in my case, one gets a bit unnerved by it.

You see that all the time now in America — more and more psychology offered and believed. I am not sure it is as satisfying as the old moral and spiritual traditions. But it is certainly witnessed by anyone who wants to watch and listen.

I have found schools that have no interest at all in religious education. Such a school can be run by someone who is not conventionally religious, but certainly is a Messianic figure if not a guru. Full of conviction about himself and his way of seeing the world, but not shy about himself and his work, and quite willing to share his personal (what would the old-fashioned word be?) charisma with others.

Now there is an old tradition to this right out of the religious and spiritual tradition so we ought not be surprised by this. The function of charism in cures and healing — that goes back biblically thousands of years, doesn't it?

One ought not necessarily put this down psychologically or, for that matter, morally. Charism can indeed touch and heal, and does. And we ought to bow to that.

I have been in institutions where, again, spirituality is more acknowledged than really sought and relied upon. I've also been in institutions where religion and the spiritual life is much addressed. What it comes down to, or up to obviously, is the conviction of the particular people involved with these children. What is one interested in? What does one think of spirituality as being? Is it the music, the hymns? Is it the message as conveyed in the Bible or in prayers? Is it some kind of group setting that is ultimately translated into the language of psychology? In other words, religion interpreted as part of one's psychological development?

One sees a whole range of attitudes. For me, the most satisfying moments — and ultimately this is what one has to offer — are those moments in which young people somehow are being addressed by others who have some personal convictions, some personal inwardness, even some personal turmoil, that fuel the way the young people are treated. Being addressed, in other words, by a moral and spiritual life on the part of the older person who is working with these young people.

How does one do this? The techniques, I argue, matter less than the individual's passion of heart, mind, and soul. And I would imagine there is a range of ways to do this, depending on who you and I are. I would think the first step ought to be our willingness in some way to put ourselves on the same plane with the other person. That we are together as fellow human beings and that we are walking on the same road of disappointment and hurt and thwarted ambition and curiosity, where knowledge is found to not be all that helpful.

That's what Malcolm X experienced in that prison. Some

brothers came to him and said, "Hey, here we are. Here we are. The whole world has contempt for us but we can in some way show ourselves, never mind them."

And this, I would suspect, is a common attribute of a successful person who can work with young people. To be able to say, "I'm with you. I too am hurt and vulnerable. I'm not going to make a federal case out of it and make you worry about me and feel that I'm some kind of a kook. But nevertheless, I'm also not going to patronize you." We can patronize people with psychology, and do so every day in the way we label them, dismiss them, write them off. Just think of what someone could have called Malcolm X — a hopeless prospect. And not only Malcolm X.

Troubled youth. Hard to be with. Hard to get to. A doctor like me comes into the room as I did on occasion after occasion. "Who are you? And what do you want from me? Another big shot? Full of information? On the prowl? Trying to learn something to further an already bloated career? Who are you? And why should I talk to you in any kind of honesty? I know your type. I know your type."

They talk this way or that way. But what do they have in common? By and large, they're for themselves. As a lot of us who teach, or practice medicine, or do counseling can occasionally be, they're for themselves. They're standoffish or they preach or they punish or they hector us with raptures and sermons. And why should we listen to that stuff? Who in our lives has given us the sense that if you listen to that stuff, it really pays off?

What we have met up with is arbitrary and cruel authority. A disappointing world. A miserable world. An unjust world. How are you going to address the matter of justice and fairness and equity with these young people? Are you going to tell them, "Hey, shape up and maybe, if you're very lucky, you'll be like me"? Talk about the culture of narcissism. Is that our message?

Or is the message: "We have some techniques here. I'm going to teach them to you. And you can become psychologists like us. And you know techniques."

Or is the message: "Get down on your hands and knees and

pray. Pray and pray. We've got the sermons for you. And don't do anything else but pray. And if you do that long enough, we'll call you reformed. We'll say that you've seen the Lord and we'll call you born again, even saved."

My hunch is that to all of those people some salt will be directed. Understandable and even good salt of skepticism — "I've heard this before" or "I know this." This is authority unearned, and authority unearned can be offered in the name of criminology, psychology, psychoanalysis, organized religion, the law, and whatever, from the point of view of many of these young people.

What kind of authority does one hope for? I would hope for the kind of authority that, as a parent, I'm trying to earn for my children. And what kind of authority is that? Ultimately, one hopes and prays it's the authority of a fellow traveler, as in John Bunyan's *Pilgrim's Progress*. It's the authority that one shares with others built on one's own hurt and vulnerability. We are — and I can only repeat this — all at risk. And to know that is maybe to know a big textbook full of psychology and medicine.

I would recommend to you Tolstoy's *Master and Man* and *The Death of Ivan Ilyich*. Those two stories illustrate Tolstoy's struggles with human vulnerability and grief and arrogance and self-importance. And those qualities can be found, by the way, in some of us called therapists or doctors or experts, not just in the children and young people we treat.

How does one somehow find meaning in this life as a lawyer? Ilyich was a lawyer. Or as a businessman as in *Master and Man*, a story of a businessman who's trying to make a deal? Sometimes when we're treating people, we're trying to make deals with them. We're trying to clinch a deal. And the other party says, "I don't want to deal with you. Who are you? I've had dealings with characters like you for years. Why should I sign up with you?"

How does one help people to share in a signature, maybe so that we're both writing, blood connected to blood? Maybe by writing our signature in blood or offering some human sweat in the confessional mode, things that Saint Augustine and Tolstoy both urge on us. In *The Death of Ivan Ilyich*, the businessman is trying to make a deal and he's dragging his servant with him through a Russian winter. Ultimately the storm takes over even as it did Napoleon and Hitler, who were after bigger deals than this poor businessman.

That is nature and life in its enormity and perplexity and unpredictability. Life wins over all of our human schemes, including the intellects. We are puzzled and in awe of life, and humbled by it and faced by it with our at-risk nature, our essential vulnerability. The jeopardy in which we all flail as we try to reach whatever shore we're struggling toward. Think of those of us who have no shore. Only process? Doing process for the rest of our lives. God save us. Let's process that.

In Tolstoy's Ilyich, the master at one moment suddenly realizes this is it. And in a revelatory moment, he understands — what is the expression — human vainglory, to draw upon the 19th century language that I suppose we'd all be embarrassed to use in our "consultative roles," as it's put with institutions.

And what does he view, this master? He sees that he will soon enough die but somehow his servant is destined to live. And the master now becomes the servant; there's a biblical tradition for this. The master becomes a servant and offers his coat to the servant. The master is humbled and doesn't lord it over that servant. He becomes with and a part of that experience. And ultimately, of course, he dies, even offering his body for warmth to that servant. It's a beautiful story. And I think it has so much to teach us about what we might do with those young people we work with. Don't scare them with an onwash of sentiments. Certainly don't hector them with various pieties, or make it our task only to figure them out psychologically. We need some sentiment occasionally and we need to be told off occasionally. And let's have plenty of psychology; I don't have to urge that on anyone these days.

But beyond that is something, I would argue, that is much more important. And it is the sensibility that we have as part of our spiritual tradition that goes back, in our time, to Dorothy Day

27

working in soup kitchens, and to Dr. Martin Luther King. And to Tolstoy's stories. And to Catherine of Siena when she said, "All the way to heaven is heaven. For Jesus said, 'I am the Way.'" This is a kind of existentialism that has been given to us by novelists, playwrights, short story writers, and poets, and which can be lived out, I would think, by us as we do our work.

Walker Percy has a wonderful moment in one of his novels. There is a character whom he describes as one of those people who got all A's and flunked ordinary living. Now, your task and mine is not only to teach psychology to our children in such a way that they would get an A in psychology and mouth back to us all these psychological pieties, but also, very candidly, to learn how to live an honorable life, sometimes helped by these children as much as we can help them. And for a young person to be told how important he or she is in our lives may be a step in that direction.

And it's important for us to acknowledge that in the course of our work, tactfully and sensibly, at the right moment, not in some crazy way of, "Well, gee, I just heard a lecture and I'm going to talk to all of you kids and tell you what the lecturer said."

It isn't a matter of what is said, anyway. It's the spirit. A spirit that is wry and ironic as Percy's was, that can point out to us that you can be very smart, including having a doctorate in psychology or psychiatry or whatever, and be a damn fool in the way you live a life. A damn fool. You may have noticed that some of these people who consult with you are damn fools. Sometimes even the people who lecture to you may occasionally be damn fools in the way they live their lives. It's one thing to give a good lecture or to write 578 books and another thing in how you are with your wife or husband, with your children, with people, fellow human beings called patients.

Do you take advantage of knowledge in order to put people down? Do you exploit the awe they feel toward you by virtue of your profession? Your age? The title that's given to you by the people who run an institution? Are you full of yourself and all too willing to have others know about it? Is the entire institution that you

28

run filled with your sense of your own perceived greatness? And are these children merely asked to become your sheep, then graduated with high honors?

These are terribly important introspective questions that I think Saint Augustine asked us to consider a long time ago. And they're questions I would hope we would consider as we go about doing our work today.

There is a long tradition of autobiographies that can help us in this regard. There is Dorothy Day's book, *The Long Loneliness: The Autobiography of Dorothy Day*. There is Thomas Merton's wonderful confessional writing, *The Seven Storey Mountain*, the last writings he did before he left us. But of course he has never left us. He is with us and so is Dorothy Day. And so are all of the people who have offered us the wisdom of stories. Like Raymond Carver's fiction in a book called, *Where I'm Calling From*. Stories of hurt and vulnerability. Of understandings, of turnings, and misunderstandings.

These stories, these personal recollections, and for that matter, all history itself, can help us as we try to link arms with those others who inhabit a Boys Town. Who was Abraham Lincoln? The issue is not cultural literacy, which is the way it's phrased to us these days, but moral literacy. The issue is not the dates of Lincoln's life and the Civil War battles and his presidency from 1860 to 1865. The issue is what kind of a person was he? And let us go beyond the idolization of the great president with a statue of him sitting on a chair in Washington, D.C. Let us connect with him. You and I. His poverty and frailty. And the mistakes he made. And his ambitions. And the disappointments. And all the troubles he had. All the troubles he had at work and at home. And the melancholy that came upon him. And bitterness. To bring him to life. A melancholy and bitterness and hopefulness that is part of everyone's life.

We all should acknowledge — including those of us who are therapists, teachers, priests, ministers, whatever — these categorizations when we are with others called at-risk youth.

Let me tell you, as helpful as these can be, there also are problems and hindrances and blind spots on our way. They herd together. They deny human particularity and individuality. They set up ratios of power and authority. They distance us from one another as well as — occasionally, one hopes and prays — help us to understand one another. It is a mixed blessing to have a mind hellbent on talk called knowledge, capital K. Indeed, just look at the history of the world.

How did William Carlos Williams put it? "Outside, outside myself, there is a world." Well, to break outside of oneself that way — to look at people candidly — is to realize that all the knowledge in the world can lead to what? It can lead to the knowledge of Ezra Pound, who was a brilliant poet and intellectual who was filled with hate. It can lead to the knowledge of Joseph Goebbels, one of Hitler's right-hand men, who had a Ph.D. in comparative literature from the University of Heidelberg — Germany's Harvard. And who was a murderer. It can lead to the knowledge that Emerson had in mind when he made the distinction in the first place, in the American vein so to speak, between character and intellect.

We are struggling with the issue of character. How does one teach others character? I would suspect one way is to learn about character within one's self. And to struggle mightily with that dilemma where one can be very bright and very well-educated and, for that matter, lack character. That's what Emerson said more than 150 years ago in big-shot Harvard when he gave that American scholar address. "You can be very, very smart," he pointed out to the audience, "not necessarily good."

Well, what is character? And how do we address it? With lots of psychological words? With sages and phases of moral development? Just think of poor Ruby and where she'd fit in that. Ruby would have been put in the preconventional stage of moral development at the age of six. Automatically. There she goes — a mere six years old — funnel her into that stage.

Who gets in the postconventional stage of moral development? Very few people. Usually, you will notice the implications of people who get in there; they're probably the people who devise these stages, along with the people with whom they choose to associate themselves. Maybe a few of their Cambridge neighbors. Most people don't get in there at all. They, as Yeats put it, "slouch toward Bethlehem."

But the fallacy in all of this is not that there's anything wrong with these stages. There isn't. The issue is what do these stages tell us? They tell us a hell of a lot about the workings of the human intellect — how you figure things out. That is, they tell about moral reasoning and its growing capacity as it is nurtured in various people who are presented with moral scenarios and then graded. This is an intellectual activity. But no theorist, I hope, has ever claimed that you can equate such development with one's progress in the lived moral life.

Just because you get an A in a moral reasoning course does not mean you're living an honorable and decent life. That's what one Harvard undergraduate pointed out to me one day when he came to my office three days after I'd been to one of the schools I was commissioned to see in the course of a project for Boys Town. He sat in that office and told me something I'd heard before from one or two of them in the course of my long years of teaching there, though not often enough. He said that he'd been getting A's in moral reasoning courses and he wasn't a very good person. And when I heard that, I thought, "I've heard this before occasionally and I know how to address it."

And I said, "Well, why do you say that?" (That's my kind of question.)

Well, after I heard what he said I thought he was right. Of course, we're not trained to say that — "You are right!" What we're trained to say is, "Well, do you want to talk a little more about this?"

So I got him to talk a little more about it. And he convinced me even more that he was right. He told me about the A's he got and the scoundrelish behavior he's capable of with his girlfriend and his roommates, and he told me of his envies, his rivalries, his jealousies. I felt like saying, "Buster, don't make a big deal out of this. It's just an ordinary moment in Saint Augustine's life and yours and mine.

But, you are a Harvard undergraduate and I'm a Harvard professor so anything that happens to us is elevated."

So we talked some more. And then, finally, I figured out a way to be therapeutic. I said to him, "Well, I guess if you've learned this here at Harvard, you've learned a lot." And he was kind of pleased with that. But only for a moment, thank God.

And he threw it right back at me. He said, "I don't think that's enough to know that." That was a very poignant moment, and that's where we connected. I said, "You're right. It isn't enough. Still, it's a beginning. If you and I know that you can con a professor or a psychologist who is presenting you with various moral scenarios, and if you can come up with the right answer and it doesn't connect with how you've lived.... Boy! This is the beginning of something."

Then he said, "Well how do you live in such a way that your ideals connect with your everyday behavior?"

"Oh, no one knows the full answer to that," I said. "On the cross Jesus felt betrayed. Defense of this life is that kind of vulnerability and that kind of asymmetry or dissonance in which professed faith, even ardently held faith, can flounder in the face of our humanity."

So even if I answer all the questions right and am declared at the highest stage of moral development, that is a testimony to my intellectual life. God bless me. And God forgive me.

So I try to figure out how to take all that stuff and all that knowledge and those degrees and that cleverness and intellectuality — and let's add to it insight and therapeutic working out and knowledge again of family life and problems — and fit it into an everyday life. That's what Ruby somehow was able to do. Even when she was six she didn't know who Sigmund Freud or Lawrence Kohlberg was. You name them.

She did know, however, not so much who Jesus Christ was, but how he lived. That was interesting to me. That's the way her parents taught her Christianity. They told her that Jesus was a carpenter, that his friends were fishermen. They didn't go to Ivy League colleges or get a Ph.D. or an M.D. or any of those other degrees. They had no

— we say it so pontifically and ominously almost — training.

Fishermen, carpenters. Jesus was friendly with all sorts of people. And a lot of them weren't popular. And everyone looked down on a lot of them. And a lot of them — let's say it right here — were at risk. They were at risk!

At-risk kids. At-risk human beings. At-risk teachers and psychologists. And Jesus, who was at risk. And all those friends of His who were at risk — the lepers and the criminals, the blind people, the lame, and the unpopular. The rebuked and the scorned. They were all at risk and so was He. And ultimately He suffered the final penalty of being at risk.

The prophets of Israel — Isaiah, Jeremiah, and Micah — were at risk, too. These were not big-shot college professors or political figures. They were utterly scorned by principalities and powers.

Please, as we go on, do not sell short the richness, the texture, the subtleties, the truths, the vitality, the moral and spiritual energy that can be found in those stories of Judaism and Christianity, and those stories, about storytellers. Our Raymond Carvers, our Tobias Wolffs, our Tolstoys, our Flannery O'Connors.

There's a wonderful story by Flannery O'Connor called, "The Lame Shall Enter First." It's a story about a psychologist and a troubled at-risk youth. And boy, is it biblically connected and filled with revelatory power. And I wish stories like that could be used in our Boys Towns and in those schools that I visited. Just as they belong in our universities, studied not only texturally and cleverly as to symbols and metaphors, but studied with heart and soul to discover the meaning and the message of that story.

Just think of what our school children now have to face. The Bible has been taken out of the classrooms. So many of us have no use for the flag. And the texts have been taken apart by all these intellectuals. And what is left? Where do we find meaning? Well, we find meaning in your and my reading of Flannery O'Connor and Walker Percy.

There are two wonderful stories by Tobias Wolff. One is called "In the Garden of the North American Martyrs." Boy, does that tell you about intellectuals and how they behave. And then there's another story called, "The Liar." It's about what you and I might call a sociopathic personality. But it's about something else. It's about how that can turn into something wondrous. It's a lovely story, told without self-consciousness.

Let us connect with stories as the Bible urges us to do; it is filled with them. And let us reach out with our own stories to others who have their stories, to these young people who can be our teachers and remind us not only about how much work has to be done with their at-risk situations, but also with our own at-risk situations.

And so, as the expression goes, so it goes.

In concluding, I can only wish you what my mother used to wish my brother and me when she pushed us off to school in the morning. She'd say one word to us. And that word was "Godspeed." And thank God it was that. I can think of other words she might have used these days, addressing her ego in the mechanisms of defense. All that was beyond her. Again, thank God. I wish you well.

*DR. ROBERT COLES, professor of psychiatry and medical humanities at Harvard University, is renowned the world over for his work in researching and recording the spiritual, moral, and political life of children. Among the dozens of books he has published are his landmark works, **The Moral Life of Children** and **The Spiritual Life of Children**. Dr. Coles served as a special consultant for the development of the Boys Town training program, "Pathways: Fostering Spiritual Growth Among At-Risk Youth." His essay in this volume was first presented at the 1993 symposium, "The Spiritual Life of At-Risk Youth: The Ongoing Journey."*

REFERENCES

Erikson, E.H. (1964). **Insight and Responsibility**. New York: Norton.

CHAPTER TWO

Some Thoughts on Religious and Spiritual Education with Vulnerable Youth

DR. ROBERT COLES

The following article also was written by Dr. Robert Coles. His insights were gleaned from his conversations with many of the young people who participated in the Lilly Endowment study, "Pathways: Fostering Spiritual Growth Among At-Risk Youth."

*A*s I went from place to place in the course of this effort (in Massachusetts, Rhode Island, New York), I began to realize how important it is to think about the relationship between psychology (psychiatry, psychoanalysis, the social sciences) and religion in this late-20th-century, heavily secular, and materialist society. Again and again (even in a setting run by the Catholic Church, and named after one of its cardinals!) I was impressed by the power, the moral authority, wielded by my profession — the way psychological thinking dominates the assumptions, values, and certainly, the language of those who work with troubled children and youth, and of course, inevitably, the young people themselves. I say this with no necessary animus, though in some instances I was, indeed, quite upset by what I regarded to be a virtual abdication of religious and spiritual concerns in favor of psychological talk — and talk and talk! After all, these were boys and girls, youths who were very much in psychological trouble, serious trouble. So why shouldn't those who work with them be as sophisticated as can be with respect to the workings of the mind, and deeply interested in sharing such knowledge with children desperately in need of insight as to why they behave as they do.

Nevertheless, even with the relatively far less disturbed people who undertake psychoanalysis — the bourgeois "neurotics" of this 20th century — that hard-earned acquisition, insight, again and again, proves not altogether as transforming as it was originally hoped to be. Erik H. Erikson, one of our great child psychoanalysts, once made a connection between "insight" and "responsibility," and amplified in this manner: "To know more and more about oneself is not necessarily to become a different person!"

When I heard him speak those words, I remembered the long disquisitions, of sorts, I used to hear from the great hero of my late teens and early twenties, Dr. William Carlos Williams, who combined a life of reflection and action by practicing medicine among New Jersey's poor, and writing poems, short stories, or novels. He was forever reminding his readers (reminding himself!) that all the talent and intelligence in the world (even psychological intelligence) doesn't necessarily translate into good, solid, decent conduct lived out daily. He had watched his brilliant poet friend Ezra Pound, so learned and wise in so many ways, become consumed by hate. And yes, he had watched some of his doctor friends in psychiatry acquire enormous psychological understanding of themselves — go on to become trained psychoanalysts, even — and yet show themselves capable of being small-minded, mean-spirited, stingy, greedy, and all too full of themselves; a wide range of human limitation, if not evil.

If all the foregoing is not an original psychological (or moral) statement, it is, yet, one we who work with troubled children need to keep in mind constantly, lest we clutch at psychiatric phrases (and formulations) as if they are God's words only to learn rather quickly that we have been clutching at straws in a contemporary wind. In one residential treatment center, for instance, I was told that "all psychological modalities" are brought to bear on the resident young people, and I tried to nod with grateful approval and enthusiasm.

When I met some of the children, I was surely impressed with the seriousness of their problems, with the "disorder and early sorrow," if not the terrible trauma, that had conspired to bring them to such an institution. Many of them talked knowingly about their "problems," their "hang-ups," even the "trauma" they had experienced. Many of them, too, had explored the "reasons" for their present situation — the difficulty, as one boy put it, "of adapting." When I asked him what he meant by adapting, he was savvy, even eloquent: "I'm in a bind. I can't get myself to be free of all the bad memories I have — my father beat me all the time, and he beat my mother, and I hear his voice in my head, and I hear him screaming at me, and I realize now it's me, it's me screaming at myself! I'm my worst enemy!" All very well and good, I think. I press on, ask him what he sees ahead for himself now, what prospects he envisions to be his. He sits, takes a sip of his Pepsi, lowers his head, then lifts it up, lets his eyes finally meet mine, and with a faint smile tells me what is in store for him during his further stay in the institution where we are both sitting: "I've got a lot more to find out about myself!"

I guess I'm supposed to be pleased with such an affirmation, proudly offered. I am sure, actually, that the boy was right. Though, of course, his comment in some fashion applied to all of us — yet another psychological banality handed down as the Lord's special wisdom. But I am not at all thrilled by what I have heard, and I make clear my misgivings this way: "What do you hope you will be doing with your life in the years immediately ahead of you?"

The boy is silent for a few seconds, then surprises me with his own question: "What do you mean?"

I thought I had made myself clear, but I agree to restate my inquiry: "What are your plans? I mean, what would you like to be in life? Where would you like to live? Have you had any ideas about the kind of work you'd like to do?"

By then I thought I'd made myself reasonably clear and had given the lad plenty of room to maneuver in a fairly open-ended, conventional asking mode. But the youth was adamant: "I can't make any decisions now; I've got some more to learn."

I was irritated enough, I fear, to press him about that response, even though I knew full well what he meant to let me know: "About what? Learn about what?"

He missed not a beat: "About myself."

I would never want to deny anyone the right to wish more and more self-knowledge. But I wondered with some dismay when this child, already in trouble because he was sullen, truculent, and all too spiteful in school and in a foster home, would ever begin to look outside himself for some inspiration, rather than look inside himself so relentlessly for a more and more subtle sense of who he was and how he had come to be who he was. He was, a bit later on, well able to explain to me why he had become a rather formidably aggressive child who caused a good deal of fear in his classmates at school, not to mention in elders such as his earnestly well-meaning, attentive foster parents and his schoolteachers. But he had no idea as to how he might learn to subdue such behavior, nor — very important — why he ought to do so. He was intent on finding out more and more about the "roots" (his word) of the "violent behavior" (his caretaker's phrase) that had been responsible for his court-ordered confinement, though he had no sense of how he might live differently and to what purpose. His mind's energies were directed inward, backward in time, an examination of a hurt, painful past. He had not been asked to look ahead or even look around at others with any real commitment of concern. I say this not with any special disapproval. I was reminded, rather, of the point of view people like me learn in our professional training, and in the course of the psychoanalytic treatment that accompanies that training: the well-known "inwardness" that takes over as we scrutinize anything and anyone so very carefully. Still, I know that boy doesn't have years to spend in such seemingly exclusive self-examination. No boy is given such a blank check of time.

He needs to be helped to make choices, to figure out what matters to him, and very importantly, to find others to trust, to hold up high. And he needs to have some sense of a world larger than that of his own mind, its memories, and ongoing experiences. I realize that his psychological sophistication, increasing as it was weekly, would ideally help in that regard. It would enable him to be more responsive to others, less angrily suspicious of them, less inclined to strike out at them, both in imitation of what he had experienced at the hands of others and as a "defensive" maneuver on his own — hit before he is himself hit. Nevertheless, I felt in him an unexpressed need for (even a yearning for) moral and spiritual direction, an intimation on my part prompted not by anything he said to me as we sat face to face, formally, in the room where I was "interviewing" him, but by this exchange as we were saying good-bye:

"Did you want to be a doctor when you were my age?"

"No."

"Did you know what you might be, then?"

"Not for sure. I thought I might want to travel a lot and see lots of places."

"I wouldn't mind traveling. But mostly, I wish I could find a place where I liked everyone, and I could decide things."

"What things?"

"Things like what I'd like to do when I'm old enough to be my own boss, and there's no one to boss me around."

How do we help such a child find some moral authority over himself, over his life — a moral authority that is not based on fear, bitterness, hate? Obviously, psychology and sociology have a lot to offer here — the everyday living arrangements and relationship that, in their sum, can help an institutionalized child learn new ways of getting on with others.

On the other hand, that boy was addressing me, who stood before him as an expert of sorts, a certified big-shot in the world of medicine and psychiatry (so he'd been told). And in essence, as we got ready to part, he was putting me under some kind of inquiring scrutiny: What had it been like for me, and very importantly, when (and by implication, how) had I made certain important choices? Put differently, he was indirectly posing the matter of will for himself by casually trying to learn about my own developing sense of commitment to things, my struggle for purpose. He, too, was hoping eventually to "decide things." And correctly, he knew already that a series of psychological traumas impeded his progress in that regard. Still, I felt in him a readiness for people other than those bearing psychological truths, for all their decided significance. I felt he required not only "insight," but also the inspiration that can come from a certain kind of teacher or coach or counselor (in his or her out-of-office everyday moments), or yes, clergyman. I do not, I hasten to add, have in mind yet another kind of psychology, the thinly veiled kind that takes religious (or even sports) language and turns it into the clinical kind. Already this boy had experienced a taste of two such turns of events: "group meetings" in which stories garnered from both the Bible and the playing field were "translated" into their "emotional meaning for the children," a phrase I heard used with understandable pride, but a phrase that worried me a good deal; and an undercutting, patronizing tone directed at the Bible or the playing field, as if they themselves were not quite worthy of a child's personal engagement.

Those who have been hurt, even betrayed, by others in childhood most urgently need to learn about the past and master its silence, but tenaciously hold it through the workings of an unfolding awareness (itself an elusive ideal, I fully realize), which is meant to give strength and healing to troubled young people in many residential or nonresidential settings. But those who have been hurt, even betrayed, need not only a vision inward, but also day-to-day reminders that in the history of the world, few have escaped pain or disappointment of one kind or another; indeed, it is our fate to be hurt and ultimately to be laid low, as it were. But it also is our fate to be able to respond, even in dire straits, to the suggestions others offer, to their example, and to the stories their lives offer us who are involved (so it might be put) in the writing of our lives.

I met a young lady (age 13) in one institution who told me she was "basically the same" now, as she was preparing to leave, as she was when she arrived months earlier. A discouraging avowal, I thought, from a person quite able, I had noticed, to be sardonic, even provocatively angry, testy, and inconsiderate. I was tempted to express my sadness in one or another brief ways ("Oh, that's too bad!") but decided in favor of silence. The young lady then qualified herself with this observation: "I was sitting in the (recreation) room watching TV, and this guy came on, and he was talking about himself. I was ready to switch the channel, but he 'caught' me. He told how he'd been beaten up all the time when he was a kid, and he was abandoned — I think his mother died and his father just walked away. That's what happened, I think. So, the guy was ready to go do anything, anything, and I guess he did. I think he was in a gang and he was into drugs. But there was this one person (also in the gang) he liked. And this person got killed. He was shot. The guy saw him dying on the street, and just before he died, the person told his friend something; he must have whispered maybe. Then the guy talking on the TV just turned around. He swore he wouldn't forget what his buddy had told him there, dying on the street, and he said on TV what his buddy had told to him. He said his buddy told him, 'Hey, please never forget that it's enough for me to die, so don't you go ahead and die this way. You let me die for both of us!' That's what the guy on television was saying, and I couldn't stop looking. Later, I could just see that guy on the street, all soaked in blood, and the life was just leaving him, leaving him real fast, but he was trying to do something; he was telling his friend something, and it was the last thing he said. And you see, the friend couldn't forget it; he wouldn't, he didn't, and that's when he changed, that's how he changed. And you know what? I'm thinking a lot about that guy on television, and I hear myself saying: 'Hey there, you could get killed, just any second you could, even if you were minding your business completely. So you should decide whether you want to end up increasing your chances or decreasing them. And you should try to listen to what that dying person said, the way the guy did on television, and I am doing so.'"

Such a remark — those last two words, in their own way a ringing existentialist affirmation — may seem to be offhand, and indeed, may seem to be an offhand consequence of an offhand experience, the kind many of us correctly have learned to shower with skepticism, if not disdain: television in all its deadening banality, and awful, stupid violence. Even so, a youth was caught unaware, perhaps caught by the dramatic, urgent, insistent story-telling confessional of someone who had been headed nowhere fast, and who had somehow been brought up short, brought to his senses, by a tragedy of tragedies: a young friend's sudden street death at the hands of a rival gang.

Such a redemptive moment for one onlooker soon enough turned into another redemptive moment for another onlooker. Jaded and "hostile" as she was, she was taken aback, moved to serious, repeated moral examination: "I guess I'd better find a way to get a better life for myself, or I could end up there (dead on the street)." The critical word in that comment, that self-remonstrance shared with a visitor, is "better" — evidence of a mind's moral energy at work. So it can go. So it can happen. And so the gloomy, cynical, resentful, and raging side notwithstanding, a street's moral moment (a dying person trying to offer his buddy a last-minute, last-time moral and spiritual message) is given, gradually, a powerfully remembered persistent life.

As I left that youth, left the building where she was staying, I wondered whether she hadn't become my teacher, maybe a teacher for many of us who struggle to figure out what to "do" with, and on behalf of, her and her kind, not to mention the young man she had watched on television. He had found a truth that changed him through his experience as a street-witness. She, in turn, had become his witness. It did occur to me, thinking of her, and of him and of his friend who was felled by a bullet, that long ago some people were told by someone that His death was quite enough, so to speak; that further suffering should be unnecessary. And thereafter, others heard what those witnesses had heard, and they too became convinced, and so it has gone in the Christian world ever since.

CHAPTER THREE

Mental Health and Conscience Functioning in At-Risk Youth

REV. CHARLES SHELTON, SJ

I'd like to share some research data, some reflections from my own writing on the area of the moral life and the interface of the Christian life, moral theology, and mental health, and also some personal reflections and clinical observations. I'm going to try to tie together both hard research and what we might call soft research, plus personal reflections.

I want you to take from this something that you can use in your own ministry or professional work with young people.

Why talk about morality or ethics in terms of spiritual life? Well, if we talk about spirituality as a relationship with some type of transcendence, it necessarily evokes questions and decisions. Those questions and decisions have to do with values and what a person should or should not do. Quite frankly, in working with young people — both disturbed adolescents and normal adolescents — I find reflecting with them on concrete moral dilemmas and situations in their lives to be very, very helpful as a springboard that allows me to then go in and talk about values, affections, and their psychic lives. The way to talk about moral development is to first talk about conscience.

First, I'd like to share some opinions. In regard to self-esteem, some data indicate high self-esteem in adolescents. I can't say I believe that. I think that may be a function of the instrument used. If we used more projective types of tests, like Rorschachs and TATs,

45

what we might find is psychological and inner poverty in a lot of these kids. I suspect that they answer these self-reports the way they do as a type of defensive functioning. If they really admitted they had low self-esteem, they would have to admit their own pain, and it's just too much for a lot of them to consider.

Second, girls were found to have lower self-esteem than boys have and that is certainly consistent with most literature on adolescence. Some of this has to do with body image. We live in a culture that really emphasizes the body. This is very burdensome for many adolescent females. It's tough growing up as an adolescent. It's even tougher being a female adolescent growing up today.

Third, in regard to prosocial behaviors, girls tend to help in relational, interpersonal areas, and boys tend to help in doing the best they can do in terms of more instrumental types of behaviors. You find that adolescent girls focus on relational issues with other girls, and boys focus more on participating in activities with other boys.

One of the biggest fears adolescents have is the death of a parent. This can be explained simply by the word "abandonment." Kids don't want to be abandoned, and of course there's this enormous affective bond between the parent and the child. I remember reading a case where a mother doused her child with gasoline and set him on fire, and when he was in the burn unit, he still cried "Mommy." That shows the power of the affective bond. This example shows that attachment is very important.

Finally, data show that kids are acting out sexually. That's very common today; it's even more so with at-risk youth. That's one area of life that a lot of kids don't like to look at. I think that it's a defense mechanism, a compartmentalization. You seal off one area of your life, and you just don't want to examine it.

The definition of at-risk kids, in my opinion, is those youth who are exposed to experiences that adversely impact their physical, emotional, intellectual, or spiritual growth. Of course, child abuse and sexual abuse are two such experiences. Some kids can weather things better than others. Some kids do have better support systems than others. Those things attenuate the adverse experiences they feel.

Another thought I have is that you cannot dichotomize spirituality and religion. I do not find such separation helpful. My personal feelings are that doing so creates a simplistic and false dichotomy. If I had to use a metaphor of how to view spirituality and religion, I'd like to think of them as being similar to an accordion. If it's stretched too far and held there, the music goes limp. There's a tension between the one side and the other. Now think of religion as one side and spirituality the other side of the accordion. When they come together, they make music. On the religious side, religion is an organizing principle and we need that. But you can take it too far and it becomes denigrating, judgmental, and punitive. Spirituality also can be taken too far. We have to self-critique everything, not only religion, but spirituality, too. Anything can be used for a corrupt purpose. On the other hand, just the right amount leads to self-understanding and insight. It makes one aware of one's own ambiguity and makes one responsible and healthy. But taking spirituality too far leads to narcissism — "my experience, me, me." So I think both religion and spirituality can be taken too far. They're both important, they go together, and I would not want to dichotomize them.

Another thought I have is about statistics. Being a mental health professional, I've done a lot of work in statistics. Certainly, statistics can lie and can be used in false ways. One of the things I have done in my writing is criticize psychology because I think that some psychologists have tried to reduce the moral life to a research study. One of my arguments is that the moral life is such a rich construct that we can't reduce it simply to statistics. This is called "the empirical fallacy."

On the other hand, we need statistics. If we are competent, we make an intervention with a kid not only because it feels right, but also because it's what we know from our own experience as well as our own study. Statistics are important because they can keep us honest. Often what happens in ministry and helping professionals is that we project our own issues on kids. The best way to ensure not projecting our own issues on children is to look at research data and what scientific data says about what we do. Even the most healthy functioning person will fall apart under severe stress. I think that's true no matter what. Mental health is a continuum, and no one has it all together. Under adverse circumstances, even the most integrative people will have difficulty.

Now I'd like to share some observations on the mental health movement today. I'm all for what's been happening in the mental health movement over the last 10 or 15 years in terms of self-help and self-help groups. That's been very helpful. But I also want to give a couple of cautions here. The first one is the use of the word "dysfunctional." It's very imprecise. That label can be used to hurt a lot of people. So we have to watch labeling. A second caution is not to use the word dysfunctional as a way of doing away with original sin or the human condition. We all have problems. Dysfunction becomes an issue when the problems we do have adversely impact on our own mental, emotional, physical, or spiritual growth. It's an idealization when we think that we can do away with dysfunctionalism. So I reject the idea that a person can change everything about himself or herself; I don't think anyone can. I also challenge the idea that a person can change nothing. We have to have a fine balance, I think.

Another idealization is the thought of the "wounded child." We'll be looking at some research that shows a child is very altruistic and very caring. But a child is also egotistical and selfish. So let's not use the image of a child as some perfect being. Another caution about the dysfunctional movement itself is that there's an awful lot of money to be made. You go into any bookstore and you have shelf after shelf of books on self-help and self-care. I'm not saying those books can't be helpful; I'm saying that anything can be taken to an extreme. Face it, there is a lot of money to be made from this literature.

Another point I want to make is that many children of alcoholics turn out very well without intervention. This is a consistent finding, and much of the scientific research we have substantiates this. That might rub against the grain of what you've experienced but many people who come from what we call dysfunctional families function okay. Of course, that depends on a lot of things — the severity of the alcoholism and other issues. But a lot of kids turn out okay.

Also, I sometimes have the feeling that this dysfunctional movement can become like a new religion. There's a politically correct way to be.

The final thing I want to say is that many people in ministry and the helping professions go into them because they themselves have come from what we would call dysfunctional families. We might too uncritically accept some of the things said in the dysfunctional literature just because of our own needs. We need to be able to discern our own projections and just accept some things uncritically.

Why study conscience? It appears that a perspective every religion and all professional disciplines agree upon is that we have something called "conscience." That suggests to me that you can use conscience in a secular setting or you can use it in a religious setting.

Second, there are some basic levels of values that we can make a commitment to. These involve characteristics such as empathy, honesty, compassion, and care. These are attributes we can challenge one another to live up to, whether in secular settings or religious settings.

Third, I've been very influenced by feminist literature, especially the work of Carol Gilligan. In her book, *In a Different Voice*, she makes a very good point when she talks about ethics of care and relational living as opposed to ethics of justice. What I try to do in my conscience construct is talk about care and compassion.

Fourth, I think we've gotten way too cognitive in what we've done in moral development. Back in the early 1950s or 1960s, we all knew what it meant to be a good Christian. You do this, this, and this; you don't do this, this, and this. Everything was set. Then after the mid-Sixties, everything just fell apart. Have you ever asked yourself the questions, "Why did things just fall apart? Why did things just break down?" No one knew what to say, no one knew what to do. That's a little oversimplified but it gets to a basic point. My answer for these questions is the following: Churches spent far too much time stressing the cognitive — do this, don't do that — and talking about rules and regulations. We didn't spend enough time talking about the affective life or the intrapsychic life. If you want to help a person grow morally, you have to take a holistic approach to the human person, which means dealing with affective, cognitive, and intrapsychic variables.

My experience is with adolescents. If you just tell them, "Do this, don't do that," and talk about moral principles and the cognitive, you put them in a situation similar to peer pressure and it's not going to work. You have to deal with issues like self-esteem. You have to deal with defense mechanisms. You have to deal with attachment, and you have to deal with guilt. These are all part of the conscience, and they're all part of healthy moral development.

A fifth reason to foster conscience, I think, is simple. What are kids going to have 10 or 15 years from now when they make moral decisions? Ideally, they'll have a supportive community church environment, of course. But realistically the one thing we do know they'll have is their conscience. They will use their conscience to make moral decisions.

Finally, in our society there is an assault on attachment, which means there's an assault on trust, an assault on the family, and an assault on compassion. I'm sure you're familiar with some of these figures, but let me just give a few of them. This is from the American Medical Association: 77 percent of eighth-graders have tried alcohol; 44 percent of tenth-graders reported riding in cars last month with someone who was drinking or on drugs; 19 percent of girls reported that someone had tried to force them into having sex. From another study: 2,740 teenagers get pregnant every day; 623 teenagers get a sexually transmitted disease every day; 1,800 children are abused every day; 3,200 children run away from home every day; 12 million children lack medical insurance. One out of five children in our society lives in poverty.

There is an assault on attachment. Many theorists are talking about the increase today of antisocial personality disorder and the increase in conduct disorder. Many psychodynamic theorists say one of the reasons for this is because there's an impaired attachment bond. With these kinds of statistics, it might give us some kind of understanding of why there's increasing fundamentalism among some youth today. If you're assaulted with abuse and venereal disease and getting pregnant, and all the consequences from the breakdown of the family, one defensive structure is to become a little more rigid in one's thinking.

Another point we should be aware of when dealing with adolescents is the issue of loneliness. The best metaphor for talking about loneliness is to use the word "hunger." What will you do if you get hungry enough? You'll do anything, right? I think that's what happens with these young kids morally; they're so lonely, they'll do almost anything to fill up that inner void. One of the best ways to talk to kids about drugs is to use the drug as an image of a best friend. What would you do for a best friend? This gets them into relational things. For a best friend you would do anything, you'd give up anything, and that's what kids who abuse drugs do. They do everything for the best friend, which is the drug. They give up their family, their school, and their other friends.

Part of conscience is biological. Some kids, according to studies on temperament, are more biologically predisposed to react than others. This has implications for a person's capacity for reflection. Part of a healthy conscience, of course, is to have reflection. So as caregivers, we just need to be aware of this biological component.

What does it mean to be a healthy adult who works with kids? First, we've got to deal with ambivalence in our own lives. Kids have a hard time dealing with ambivalence because they want to see everything in an ideal way; it makes it safe for them. We must ask ourselves what our capacity for ambivalence is. Are we able to see the positive and the negative in our own love relationships, for example, and in the things we do in our own lives? Kids can't tolerate ambivalence as easily as adults do. Helping kids understand ambivalence is crucial.

Second, we need to be able to forgive our own parents.

Third, we have to be able to deal with loss.

Fourth, we have to deal with our own tendencies for regression. Adolescents bring up a lot of issues about sexuality and authority. We need to be aware of any regressive tendencies we might have.

Fifth, we have to have appropriate boundaries. You're not going to be able to save every adolescent even though you might want to. We've got to be able to admit and live with this reality.

Sixth, we need to have healthy adult relationships. Again, adolescents are notoriously strong in the capacity to make adults regress. Having healthy adult relationships (that have nothing to do with kids) helps keep a proper perspective on our own lives.

Seventh, we need to have hobbies or creative activities. This is crucially important for healthy adult living. We need to have creativity to fulfill our lives.

Eighth, we need to have a theology of friendship. If you want to work with kids, especially in the terms of value dimension, you need to have a theology of friendship. Can you articulate that, can you talk about that with other adults? When you talk about theology of friendship, you talk about love, about confidentiality, about forgiveness. Kids need to hear that from us and how we work those things out in our minds.

Ninth, we need a theology of gratitude. What are you grateful for? And what do you want to do when you feel grateful? Most of us want to give ourselves back in service. Gratitude also allows us to feel hopeful and good about something. I remember working with a girl named Ann who'd been sexually abused by four or five men, including her father. Her mother died on the operating table. I had about 70 sessions with her. It dawned on me toward the end that she saw everything in a dark way. But even Ann could deal with some grateful things — our relationship, how I esteemed her, a smile from a friend, a letter from someone, something that happened on the hospital ward. We have to foster gratitude in kids and help them realize the grateful moments in their lives. Gratitude offers hope. When you feel grateful, you want to offer service to others.

Finally, we need to talk about St. Paul's theology of gifts. We each have our gifts and we need to help encourage kids to think of their own gifts. We don't have to be perfect; we're certainly not going to be. But we do need to think about the things we can give to others that make them feel better.

In a related matter, when we look at the people we've ministered to, whether they're adolescents, children or adults, can we see them as gifts given to us? This is crucial. Once we see someone as a gift that's been given to us, it transforms that person into someone very precious. This leads us to do everything we can to nurture that person in a healthy way. So the question isn't what we do for them. It's what they do for us and how we're able to see them as gifts. The people I've ministered to in my life as a priest have done much more for me than I've ever done for them. I need to consciously realize this and talk about it. If we don't, then we get into a role relationship where we might have all the power.

Conscience can be defined as making decisions for other-centered values. One aspect of conscience is making decisions, and it has a specifically altruistic, compassionate flavor to it. Conscience incorporates affective, cognitive, and intrapsychic components. Conscience includes a cognitive factor — reasoning — which is very important, but it also includes an affective factor — emotion — and includes intrapsychic factors or internal processes.

I'd like to present my own theory of conscience. I hope you can use this theory in your work. I have a seven-dimensional view of conscience. (See chart on following page.)

I came up with this model based on my own clinical work, readings, and my discussion with several other psychologists and psychiatrists. I asked them to talk about the moral life from a psychological perspective. What does it mean to make moral decisions? What would be the factors necessary for making moral decisions? I came up with these seven factors.

My theory is that as we work on each of these seven dimensions with a child or adolescent, we can help him or her grow in his or her capacity to make moral decisions. In other words, when you're

Developmental Features of Conscience Formation

(Adapted from Charles Shelton's *Morality and the Adolescent*, page 105)*

Adolescence ➤ ➡ ➡ ➡ ➡ Adulthood

DIMENSION	POLARITIES (Some Examples)	ADULT CHARACTERISTICS
Psychic Energy	Adaptive (healthy attachments, openness, mastery of developmental tasks)	Flexibility, generative
	Nonadaptive (fixations, dissipates energy)	Unfocused, distracted, regressive
Defensive Functioning	Mature (healthy adaptive functioning)	Adaptable, realistic
	Immature (inability to cope with conflict, unrealistic view of self and the world)	Rigid, erratic, stress, immature
Empathy	Care (sensitivity, compassion)	Compassionate, caring life stance
	Insensitive (Insensitivity, compulsive care giving, overempathizing)	Isolated, insensitive, clinging
Guilt	Moral (humility, increasing self-honesty)	Integrity, humble stance
	Superego (poor self-image, self-worry)	Self-punishing, doubt, tension, rigid
Idealization	Hope (realistic optimism, goal seeking, ideal to live by)	Optimism, hopefulness, self-satisfaction
	Overidealizing (unrealistic aspiration, egotistical, critical)	Chronic dissatisfaction with self and others
Self-esteem	Inner goodness (realistic self-worth, self-honesty)	Self-confidence, gratefulness
	Inadequacy (inferiority, overcompensating)	Pervasive feelings of inadequacy
Teleology	Purposeful (responsible, reflective)	Mature moral reasoning (self-direction)
	Diffuse (unable to take responsibility, inability to articulate moral stance)	Lack of reflective value system

*From Charles Shelton, SJ, *Morality and the Adolescent*, 1989. New York: Crossroads. Used with permission of author.

working with kids who face moral decisions, think of these seven dimensions. Sometimes you might want to work with one dimension, sometimes another. But I think these are the seven dimensions to consider. It's somewhat of a psychodynamic model, and that's the bias I have; for example, dealing with psychic energy and defensive functioning. Again, my thesis is that if these seven dimensions are well-functioning in a young person, then that youth is apt to make healthy moral decisions for other-centered values. To the extent that they're not functioning well, he or she probably will not make healthy moral decisions.

Some of the themes that go with these dimensions are attachment, adaptability, and flexibility. There also is a polarity. There's a healthy and unhealthy dimension to each side.

The first dimension is psychic energy. It's the fuel, the psychological fuel, for adaptive healthy functioning. The questions we need to ask when working with a kid are: "What takes up his or her time? What does this kid attend to? How does this adolescent allocate his or her attention?"

In order to have a healthy conscience, we have to deal with appropriate developmental tasks. Healthy moral development goes hand in hand with healthy human development. If one of the things you want is for a kid to behave morally, then he or she just has to deal with basic developmental tasks. Some of the developmental tasks basically center around the physical. In early adolescence, developing the "self" and beginning to explore a philosophy of life are important. Getting to middle and late adolescence, acquiring knowledge of the world, defining oneself as a man or woman, and building commitment in relationships and vocational choice are important. In other words, just doing healthy developmental things is part of the moral life. Someone who attends to developmental tasks is most likely going to have healthy friendships. And these healthy friendships bring up all types of issues — confidentiality, violations of trust, self disclosure, empathy, care — that are integral to the moral life. Ask yourself, "What does this kid attend to in terms of his or her energies? Are they healthy, appropriate developmental paths?" If you can't find answers to those questions, you've probably got a kid whose moral decisions are problematic.

A second thing about psychic energy, besides the attention factor, is that it's limited; you only have so much. A kid who spends too much time abusing drugs or watching too much TV is going to be engaged in activities that are problematic for his moral growth. He's going to be lacking the reflectivity needed for healthy relationships, and the solitude and time needed to be alone to work through moral issues. Thus, think of it in terms of a limited amount of psychic energy. We have to define ourselves in terms of commitments to doing certain things and not doing other things. A kid who has healthy attachments and openness, and who masters developmental tasks will grow up to be an adult who will be flexible and focused. One who doesn't will fixate, dissipate energy, be unfocused or distracted, and be regressive as an adult.

The second dimension is the need for healthy defenses. There are a number of unhealthy defenses that adolescents employ. If you want to talk about the moral life, you better talk about the defenses kids use. What limited research there is on defenses says that at-risk kids use more primitive or unhealthy defenses. Sexually abused kids, for example, are into displacement and denial. Why do people have defenses? They use defenses as a way to build up self-esteem, to feel good about themselves, and to view themselves as moral persons. Even gangsters have a code they live by. It's a sick code, but they have one. Minimization, of course, is a way of downgrading something — telling oneself that stealing something wasn't that bad. Totalism is getting so involved in something that you can't look at other things. It's a basic security issue. You even see this in normal kids — the editor of the school newspaper, the athlete, the scholar. All he or she thinks about is athletics or the school newspaper or grades. Externalization is saying, "He made me do it; she made me do it." Inhibition is not taking a moral risk. Unfortunately, many at-risk kids use the next defense — acting out. They act out their conflicts and rationalize them by making excuses. Compartmentalization and stereotyping are other defenses. Why do people stereotype? It's because they're fearful; they're scared. Kids are very scared; they're scared of the unknown. They'll label other kids, other ethnic groups, other classes, and other schools. They denigrate the victim. We always need to ask what defenses a kid is using.

What are some of the more healthy defenses? They are sublimation, humor, role flexibility, and suppression. Sublimation, of course, is channeling one's aggressive and sexual urges into creative tasks. A sense of humor, of course, also can always be used in the passive aggressive way. Role flexibility is the ability to adapt oneself, to some degree, to a particular situation. Suppression has a pejorative connotation, but it's the ability to control our own impulses. Another defense is realistic anticipation. We can anticipate the future, plan ahead, and not wait until the last minute. A kid who engages in these healthy defenses is going to get positive affirmation from peers, and probably will be more well-liked by adults.

The third dimension is the use of empathy. Empathy can be viewed as the vicarious arousal to the pain and hurts of others. It's a response one has inside after seeing another person who is hurting. If you think of a flower as the moral life, the foundational soil that nurtures the flower is empathy. You can't be a moral person without being empathic. Emotion is the foundation of the moral life. Cognition is very important, moral principles are important, but it's emotion that energizes us to act morally. The moral heroes in our lives have deep-felt moral principles. Take Martin Luther King Jr., for example. He had moral principles, but he also had a passion. The reason we admired him was because he had both. It's important to talk about empathy because in terms of social justice, that's what makes someone feel a sense of compassion for the poor and the oppressed. The foundational aspect of helping is empathy. If we nurture our empathic urges, we become more caring. As psychologist Martin Hoffman suggests, the last stage of empathy allows one to embrace other groups and other cultures. Empathy is also important with regard to burnout. We have to be aware of our capacity to become overly stressed. What causes burnout? What especially causes burnout in those who work in social justice areas? Well, think about it this way: If empathy is an arousal to the pains and hurts of others and you're in a situation where you see lots of people hurting — where there has been sexual abuse, battered women, poverty, and so on, and you can't do anything about it, and you're powerless and churning inside at the pains and hurts of others — what do you think is going to happen to you over time? Your system is going to shut down. Empathy gives us insight into why people burn out. It also should be pointed out that one can overempathize. That's why boundaries are very important for caregivers. One person with excellent boundaries was Jesus Christ. He found time to party, He found time to get away and pray, and He found time to be in solitude.

I'd like to discuss the relationship of theology, empathy, and the moral life. If you look at the Good Samaritan parable in Luke 10, it says, "Jesus was moved to pity." What this talks about is Jesus being deeply moved with emotion. In Luke 10:37, it says, "He had mercy." Mercy is compassion. So if you take these two together — the deep emotional arousal and the compassion — you have empathy. What developmental psychologists are talking about and what Scripture talks about is that the Jesus we know and the Good Samaritan were empathic people. They were true to their own humanity. There is a marvelous fusion of what we're doing today in psychology and what theology says. The basic care of the Gospels is that of empathy, nurtured, of course, by Christian ideals and values. They do go together.

The fourth dimension is guilt. There is an issue here because so many caregivers have been ravaged by guilt in their own lives. They don't like to talk about guilt and sometimes have a kind of a knee-jerk reaction sometimes. Yet, guilt is essential for the moral life. There's nothing wrong with guilt. Guilt's great, if it's healthy guilt! Healthy guilt is feeling a sense of distress when I commit a wrong behavior, or fail to do something I should have done. But there also is a sense, of course, of punitive guilt; it's what I call "superego guilt." It leads to poor self-image and self-doubt. That's when I overreact and take responsibility for everybody, or when I make a situation that isn't that bad worse than it is, or when I think I should have done something when it really wasn't my issue. I find the best way to work with adolescents here is helping them experience guilt so it can be internalized in a positive way.

The fifth dimension of conscience is idealization. I think this is crucial because in morality, we talk too much about "don'ts" — a negative morality — don't do this, don't do that. I think we would do a lot better if we talked about more positive things. Ask youth questions like, "What do you dream for?", "What are your deepest desires?", "What are you becoming?", "What are the images that guide your life?" The one thing we need to do with at-risk youth, and all adolescents, is to help them think of positive images. That's why Jesus Christ becomes so important; that's why our own life stories become so important. We need to prudently self-disclose at appropriate times. We need to talk about people who have meant something to us. What are the positive images that nurture your life, those that inspire hope, and optimism, and a sense of self-satisfaction? I think too much of morality, church morality, has said, "You're bad. Don't do that." I think we need to focus more on this positive way of looking at morality.

Self-esteem is the sixth dimension. This is one dimension you can use all the time with at-risk youth. It never fails. What do I mean by self-esteem? I mean a felt sense of inner goodness, or self-appreciation. We all do things we regret when we're needy. So one issue you want to address when working with kids is their level of self-esteem. It can be said that some kids' self-esteem is so ravaged, they're so empty inside, that we do basically what I call remedial work. Someone says, "Well that's not talking about morals." I say, sure it is. Because how's someone going to be moral if they don't have a healthy sense of self-esteem? What are they going to do as adults if they don't have a healthy sense of self-esteem? They're going to engage in acting-out behaviors, or they're going to become compulsive caregivers, doing things to fill themselves up, to make themselves feel good.

Finally, I don't want to dismiss the seventh dimension of conscience — teleology. What does teleology mean? It's a philosophical term that means I take responsibility for my life, or the sake for which I do something or why I do what I do; what are the moral principles behind what I do? Certainly at-risk youth need moral principles; it's a necessary and vital structure for them.

In sum, what I ask you to do in your work with adolescents is to think of conscience in terms of these seven dimensions when ministering to youth.

THE REV. CHARLES SHELTON, SJ, is a clinical psychologist on the faculty of Regis University in Denver, Colorado. His writings include, **Adolescent Spirituality; Morality and the Adolescent;** *and* **Morality of the Heart** *(all published by Crossroads). His insights into moral development of the adolescent provide a framework within which to understand and respond to the needs of adolescents. His essay in this volume was presented at the 1991 symposium, "Facilitating Spiritual Growth Among At-Risk Youth."*

REFERENCES

Gilligan, C. (1982). **In a different voice**. Cambridge, MA: Harvard University Press.

CHAPTER FOUR

Facilitating Spiritual Growth Among At-Risk Youth

DR. DAVID ELKIND

*I*n his book entitled *The Varieties of Religious Experience,* William James made a distinction between what he called personal religion and institutional religion. Personal religion involves whatever is "personal, pure and simple" as opposed to religion that is "second hand" and based on tradition. Therefore, the potential for personal religion and personal spirituality is a constant guaranteed by our human nature. How that personal spirituality is realized, however, depends very much on the society and culture within which a young person is reared. In contemporary American society, institutional support for a young person's spirituality is weak, just at the time when his or her need for such spirituality, as a positive risk factor, is greater than it was in earlier generations.

Accordingly, in this paper I first want to briefly summarize the development of spontaneous, personal religion. Next I will describe three risk factors that are contributing to the high rate of dysfunctional behavior among today's young people. Third, I will give the major reason why, in my opinion, institutional religion is no longer a positive risk factor in promoting spirituality. I will close with a few suggestions on how institutional religion can do more to be a positive influence on young people.

In order to assess children's private, or personal, religion, it is necessary to ask them questions that catch them unaware and elicit what Piaget calls their "spontaneous" convictions. In constructing these questions, I started with remarks I had overheard children make when I was working in public and parochial schools. For example, I heard one child ask another, "If I go to church will I be Catholic?" This led to the question, "How do you become Catholic, Protestant, or Jewish?" Another time I heard a child whose cat was sick say that his dog was "praying for her to get better." This led to the question, "Can a dog or a cat be Catholic, Protestant, or Jewish?" The other four questions in the interview are similar to these questions.

Because I was a young investigator without grant funds, I did all of the interviewing myself. I talked to more than 700 Catholic, Protestant (Congregational), and Jewish (Conservative) children ranging in age from five to sixteen. I interviewed the Catholic children in Catholic schools and the Protestant children in their church on Sunday mornings while they were attending Sunday school. The Jewish children were interviewed while they were attending a summer camp. I manually recorded the interviews and then analyzed the data for systematic age trends. For all three groups, three stages in the development of religious identity were clearly in evidence (Elkind, 1962; Elkind 1963; Elkind, 1961).

At the first stage, usually ages five to seven, the child had only a global, undifferentiated conception of his or her denomination as a kind of proper name. Although he or she acknowledged being Catholic, Protestant, or Jewish, the child confused these names with terms for race and nationality:

Sid
Q. What is a Jew?
A. "A man."
Q. How is a Jewish person different from a Catholic?
A. "Cause some people have black hair and some people have blond."

Mel
Q. What is a Jew?
A. "A man."
Q. How is a Jewish person different from a Catholic?
A. "He comes from a different country."
Q. Which one?
A. "Israel."

Furthermore, at this stage the child regarded having a denominational name as incompatible with possessing a racial or national designation:

Al
Q. Can you be an American and Protestant at the same time?
A. "No, well, only if you move."

Til
Q. Can you be an American and Protestant at the same time?
A. "No."
Q. Why is that?
A. "You are not supposed to have two."

At the second stage, usually ages seven to nine, children displayed a concrete but differentiated conception of their religious denomination. Their conception was concrete in the sense that they employed observable features or actions to define their denomination. At the same time, their conception was differentiated because they discriminated among different articles and actions in order to distinguish among people of different denominations. They also used concrete features such as living with the family or barking in church to decide whether dogs or cats could have a denomination.

Mae
Q. What is a Jew?
A. "A person who goes to Temple or Hebrew school."

Bill
Q. What is a Catholic?
A. "He goes to Mass every Sunday and goes to a Catholic school."

Ron
Q. Can you be a Catholic and Protestant at the same time?
A. "No."
Q. Why not?
A. "Cause you couldn't go to two churches."

Alf
Q. Can a dog or a cat be a Protestant?
A. "Yes, because he belongs to the family.... well, maybe not because the minister wouldn't let him into church; he barks a lot."

At this stage, young people said that you could have a nationality and a religion at the same time. But their explanations were concrete to the effect that, "You can live in America and go to church" or "I am an American and a Protestant."

At the third stage, usually ages 10 to 12, young people gave evidence of an abstract, differentiated conception of their denomination. It was an abstract conception in the sense that these preadolescents no longer defined their denomination by mentioning names or observable activities, but rather by referring to nonobservable mental attributes such as belief and understanding:

Bi
Q. What is a Catholic?
A. "A person who believes in the truths of the Roman Catholic Church."
Q. Can a dog or a cat be a Catholic?
A. "No, because they don't have a brain or an intellect."

Sed

Q. What is a Jew?

A. "A person who believes in one God only, and doesn't believe in the New Testament."

When I asked third-stage preteens whether they could be American and their religious denomination at the same time, they usually replied that one was a "religion" and the other a "nationality" and that they were not the same thing. It was only at this stage that young people themselves introduced the abstract concept of "religion."

In summary, young children's conceptions of their religious denominations are vague and global and they tend to think of them as general names. School-age children gradually come to understand their denomination in a more differentiated yet concrete way. At this stage, religious identity is primarily a matter of action, of what church you go to. It is only in the preadolescent years that young people begin to understand their religious denominations as signifying a unique belief system.

Young adolescents often seem to break with the institutional religion they are part of as they are brought up. As children they obediently attend religious school and religious services with their parents. As young adolescents, however, they strongly resist participating in these activities. Such observations are in marked contrast with our findings regarding the development of children's religious denomination and prayer. In both cases we found that, if anything, personal religion becomes deeper and more profound by early adolescence (Elkind & Elkind, 1962). This suggests that in early adolescence, the young person does not become less religious but rather puts his or her faith in personal religion to the exclusion of institutional religion.

To test this hypothesis — that young people have a strong sense of personal religion in early adolescence — we undertook a study of the religious experiences of young teenagers. We assumed that religious experiences were of two general types: recurrent and unique.

Recurrent experiences are those that are habitual and to some extent consciously chosen and engaged in, such as church attendance. Unique experiences are one-time events that are unusual and unexpected, such as an accident, a death in the family, or a powerful aesthetic experience.

To assess the extent of pre-adolescents' familiarity with these two types of situations, we asked 144 ninth-grade students (ages 13 to 15) to compose two paragraphs in response to these two questions: a) When do you feel closest to God? and b) Have you ever had a particular experience when you felt particularly close to God? We read over the young people's brief essays and found that young people clearly distinguished between recurrent and unique religious experiences.

There were six different recurrent situations during which young people felt closest to God. In order of frequency these recurrent situations were: church situations, solitary situations, anxiety and fear situations, worry situations, prayer situations, and moral action situations. We also found five different unique situations. In order of frequency these were: appreciation situations (thanking God for something), mediation situations (in which God was believed to have intervened to help), initiation situations (confirmation, Bar or Bat Mitzvah), lamentation situations (in connection with a death — "God must have wanted her so he took her."), and revelation experiences ("It was a beautiful day, the flowers were in bloom, the birds were singing, the sky was blue and the sun warm, the earth smelled good and I suddenly felt very close to God.").

These results did not support the observation we began with, namely that young teenagers tend to reject institutional religion. Of the recurrent religious experiences, the most frequent were those associated with church attendance. These experiences are coupled with strong experiences of personal religion.

From these findings one might conclude that young people's disaffection with institutional religion in early adolescence is perhaps more social than it is religious. That is to say, while there may be little or no diminution of religious commitment, there is a need to distance oneself from the family and its activities as a show of growing independence. Put differently, the young adolescent's disaffection with the church or synagogue may be more a matter of growing independence rather than a lessening of religious experience or involvement.

Although young people today experience the same varieties of religious experience as young people in the past and develop their conceptions of their religious denomination the same way young people did in the past, the world about them has changed. We need to address those changes now.

Perhaps without fully realizing it, we have moved into a postmodern era wherein the fundamental beliefs of modernity — progress, universality, and regularity — have been challenged (Elkind, in press). In particular, the belief that the nuclear family is the ideal end product of an evolutionary process has been attacked as a myth that conceals much unhappiness and abuse. Divorce has become socially acceptable as have a variety of kinship forms, from single parenting to remarried families. In addition, the second sexual revolution since the 1960s has made premarital sex among nonmarried adults the rule rather than the exception.

These and many other postmodern changes have increased the power of three major risk factors on contemporary youth (Elkind, 1984). One of these is freedom. When liberated adults engage in premarital sex, they set an example for youth. The rates of sexual activity among teenagers have exploded. Some 72 percent of high school seniors are no longer virgins. The rates of venereal disease and teenage pregnancy have rocketed up along with the rates of sexual activity. There also is a new freedom and availability involving drugs, and many sixth-graders get initiated into alcohol with wine coolers.

A second postmodern risk factor is that of loss. First, the high rate of divorce means that more than half of all young people, by age 18, will have lived in a single-parent home. After divorce, more than a third of the children in the affected families never see the absent parent, usually the father.

Second, young people are losing their friends. More than 10,000 teenagers die each year in substance abuse-related car accidents. More than 5,000 teenagers kill themselves every year. Finally, an increasing number of teenagers are murdered by their peers. Recently, in a small, well-to-do suburb of Boston, two young men entered a social studies class and shot and killed another young man. Similar atrocities occur all across the country. Funerals for teenagers have become commonplace.

A final risk factor is failure. The postmodern emergence of a global economy and of international competition has dramatically altered our industrial base. Downsizing and restructuring have meant massive layoffs of middle managers and professionals, usually the most secure positions within society. Comparisons that show our students' academic achievements falling behind those of students from other countries have heightened the sense of competition and of failure. Although some of this concern is proving to be exaggerated — witness Japan's and Germany's current troubles — the pressure on young people to achieve academically has been fierce. At the same time, there has been increasing neglect of the "forgotten half," the 50 percent of young people who do not go on to higher education. For these young people, the feelings of failure are intense.

Postmodern adolescents are thus more at risk than previous generations because they enjoy more freedoms, experience more loss, and suffer more failure than did earlier generations.

One of the momentous changes in our society that has come about as a result of the postmodern critique of modernity is a shift from unilateral to mutual authority in most of our social institutions. In the modern era, for example, there was great respect for people of high political office, such as the president. People were loathe to criticize Franklin Roosevelt or Dwight Eisenhower. In industry, management was top down and chief executive officers wielded unchallenged unilateral authority. The church, too, was respected in this way. Catholics did not challenge the Pope and Protestants did not challenge the status quo. Professionals like lawyers and doctors also were respected and neither their judgment nor their morals were challenged.

Much of this changed in the 1960s and 1970s as a result of the Vietnam War, Watergate, the civil rights movement, and the women's movement. The touted individual freedom of modernity turned out to be freedom for the white, Anglo-Saxon male, not for all of society's members. Unilateral authority increasingly gave way to mutual authority. One result was the loss of respect accorded people of high office, including the president. The loss of respect now extends to corporations where bottom-up, rather than top-down, management and sharepower is becoming the rule. CEOs are now accountable to their boards, and many are being fired. With respect to religion, many Catholics now challenge the Pope's dicta on abortion. Many Protestant and Jewish denominations now accept women into the ministry and rabbinate. People have lost a great deal of respect for doctors and lawyers as they have been pilloried in the press for patient abuse, dishonesty, and malpractice. While unilateral authority still exists, it has been greatly reduced and replaced by mutual authority.

Something similar has happened in the postmodern — what I term — permeable family. The modern nuclear family was governed by a set of contracts regarding freedom-responsibility, achievement-support, and loyalty-commitment, laid down and reinforced by parents. Eventually these contracts were internalized by children and constituted their essential socialization. In the postmodern, permeable, busy coming-and-going family, contracts have been replaced by lists and schedules. While lists and schedules are useful and teach children responsibility, they are mutual rather than unilateral. A child, for example, may remind a parent of what is on the list or schedule.

The problem is that at a time in our history when young people are overwhelmed with the mutuality of more freedoms, of experiences with loss, and of competitive failure, they need more unilateral authority, not less. Thus, the mutual authority orientation of the postmodern world, in effect, adds another risk factor to those already contributing to the dysfunctions manifested by contemporary youth.

One thing we cannot do is turn the clock back. We will not undo the second sexual revolution or the shrinking of the number of nuclear families. What we can do is refurbish, to some extent, unilateral authority in the home and in the church and synagogue, as well as in other social institutions. Mutual authority is important, but leadership is important as well. The problem is how to apportion the two. In general, adolescents need adults to exercise unilateral authority when it comes to values, manners, and morals, and adolescents themselves need to exercise mutual authority in matters of style and taste. We cannot and should not dictate to young people what kind of clothes they should wear, what kind of food they should eat, or the kind of music they should listen to. On the other hand, we should ensure that an adult is somewhere in the house when teenagers are having a party and that no alcohol is available.

With respect to the church and synagogue, youth ministry is one important outreach program that is growing and that extends benevolent unilateral authority to youth. And it is all-important for youth leaders to appreciate how necessary it is for them to exercise such authority. They must state their own position clearly and decisively with respect to sexual activity, substance abuse, foul language, and pornography. Some youth workers tell me that they want to be friends with their teenagers and do not want to exert unilateral authority for fear of being associated with the adult world that young people reject. I believe that this is a mistake, and that youth leaders must be leaders. That does not mean proselytizing to our point of view, but only making clear where we stand and why.

Our society is beginning to recognize the need for caring, balanced, unilateral authority. Many universities around the country are going back to *in loco parentis* — acting in place of the parents. Specially appointed administrators help organize activities for students that reflect student interests but are monitored by adults. In high schools, volunteer programs are now mandated in many communities. The school, in a unilateral fashion, says that young people must contribute to the community. Work-study programs, apprenticeship programs, and youth work programs established by the federal and local governments all speak to the recognition that young people need more unilateral authority.

When adult society exercises unilateral authority with care and concern and in the best interests of youth, it re-establishes youth's respect for unilateral authority in general. And respect for such authority is essential to healthy spirituality. When young people feel there is no higher authority they can respect and regard with both love and apprehension, they cannot experience a full sense of spirituality. With their respect for unilateral authority reinstated, however, a negative risk factor is transformed into a positive one. A renewed spirituality, buffered by unilateral respect, will help young people better cope with the postmodern risks of freedom, loss, and failure.

DR. DAVID ELKIND, PHD, is a professor of Child Study at Tufts University. He is well known for his landmark books **The Hurried Child** *and* **All Grown Up and No Place to Go***. Dr. Elkind's essay in this volume was first presented at the 1991 symposium on "Facilitating Spiritual Growth Among At-Risk Youth."*

REFERENCES

Elkind, D. (1961). The child's conception of his religious denomination. I: The Jewish child. **Journal of Genetic Psychology, 99**, 2059-2225.

Elkind, D. (1962). The child's conception of his religious denomination. II: The Catholic child. **Journal of Genetic Psychology, 101**, 185-193.

Elkind, D. (1963). The child's conception of his religious denomination. III: The Protestant child. **Journal of Genetic Psychology, 103**, 291-304.

Elkind, D. (1984). **All grown up and no place to go**. Reading, MA: Addison-Wesley.

Elkind, D. (in press). **The postmodern family: A new imbalance**. Cambridge, MA: Harvard University Press.

Elkind, D., & Elkind, S.F. (1962). Varieties of religious experience in young adolescents. **Journal for the Scientific Study of Religion**, 102-112.

James, W. (1902). **The varieties of religious experience**. New York: Longmans.

Multicultural Perspectives

CHAPTER FIVE

Sometimes Even God Needs Help

SR. VERONICA MENDEZ, RCD

In discussing the view of the dominant culture from the
Hispanic-Latin perspective, the first thing I would like to
get out of the way is the label "Hispanic/Latino." Those
of us who come from Spanish-speaking cultures are having a hard time figuring out what to call ourselves. This is because
no term adequately reflects the reality of our situation. Though we
all come from cultures that speak Spanish, there are 22 different cultures. And because ultimately, the mother culture of us all is Spain,
there is much that unites us. Our histories of the past 500 years,
however, are unique and so there is also much that makes us different. That is why it is difficult to find one term that fits all of us. It is
similar to the difficulty of finding a title for the white, non-Hispanic
population of our country. Whites are mistakenly called "Anglos."
But what is an Anglo?

Anglo to me is someone who comes from England, from
Anglo-Saxon roots. Many in the Roman Catholic church in this
country have Irish roots, and have spent centuries fighting the
Anglos. A French person, or people of French descendants, are not
Anglo. I'm not sure the Germans are Anglos; maybe there is some
Saxon in there. And Italians, if they are anything, are Latins. Anglos
just don't fit there.

However, we have to call ourselves something. And it was
Father Virgilio Elizondo who reflected that it is only in this country

that we can be Hispanic. None of us is Hispanic in our own countries. There, we are Puerto Rican or Colombian or Cuban. But I will use Hispanic for this article. It is inadequate, but for me, it is better than Latino.

When you speak of Hispanic culture, you are speaking about the spirituality of the Hispanic because the Hispanic culture is religious and our religion is cultural.

In his book, *Pastoral Counseling Across Cultures*, David Augsburger says, "Culture marries theology, theology reflects culture." So as I speak about Hispanic culture, I am speaking on Hispanic spirituality.

What is the view our Hispanic people have of dominant culture, especially from the point of view of the young? To help answer that question, let me tell a story. I am a great believer in the power of stories. I could give you some sociological data that would answer the question but I think a story will stay with you better than any data I could provide.

This story comes from a wonderful book, *Rain of Gold*, by Victor Villasenor. (Many of the stories I share with you in this article come from this book.) It's the true story of the author's family. He starts in Mexico during the Mexican Revolution and tells the story of his family as they migrate up to the United States, running away from the difficulties of the Revolution. As with many families that migrate to a different country amid the chaos of a civil war, they get separated and they lose one another.

The father of the author, Juan Villasenor, ended up in Montana. His mother and some of his sisters and their families eventually end up in Los Angeles. As the years go by, they finally connect and Juan works his way to Los Angeles. This is where we pick up the story. (The following text is from *Rain of Gold*.)

> Juan had been home a few days before he realized how truly poor his family was and how rundown their two little houses were. He bought hammers and nails and got some roofing paper and fixed their roofs. Luisa's

children, Jose and little Pedro, helped.

Jose was an excellent worker, and Juan and his two nephews talked as they worked. Jose wanted to know about Mexico and especially about his real father, Jose Luis, whom he had never met.

"Was he a good hombre?" asked the boy.

"The best," said Juan. "A real macho a las Todas! Big and strong and slow-moving and he never lost his temper or got impatient when things went wrong."

"Tell me," said Jose, chewing his food in the big mouth-rolling, lazy-dog action his father had always done, "is it true that we were once a big powerful familia back in Mexico, tio?"

"Yes," said Juan.

"But not rich, huh?" said Pedro.

"Why do you say that?" asked Juan.

"Because Mexicans are always poor, right?" said Pedro.

"No, not necessarily," said Juan. "Mexicans sometimes have money too, Pedro. But we didn't. We had land and livestock and fields of corn."

"See, I told you," said Pedro laughing at his brother. "Mexicans can't be rich! That's all bull what Mama has been telling us."

"What?" said Juan.

"Nothing," said Jose, giving his seven-year-old brother the mean eye. "It's just that, well, when Mamagrande and Mama tell us of the past, Pedro and I sometimes..., well, can't really believe them."

"Oh, I see," said Juan. "So you don't believe your own blood, huh? But you do believe the gringos, huh? That only gringos can be rich, huh?"

"Well, that's all we have ever seen," said Pedro. "Not one Mexican in all the valley has even a good car."

Juan took a deep breath. "Oh, I see. So when your

Mamagrande and your mother tell you of Don Pio, who fought alongside Benito Juarez, and Jose the Great, who defended us from the Revolution for over four years, you doubt them?"

The two boys could see their uncle was getting angry.

"Well do you? Answer me."

The two boys nodded. And tears came to Pedro's eyes.

Juan looked from one nephew to the other. He didn't know what to do. Never in a thousand years would he have believed that the flesh and blood of his great Don Pio would come to doubt the worth of their own familia. He got to his feet and walked away before he strangled his two nephews. Oh. He was crazy, loco, raging mad. He and his mother and sister had suffered so much, and for what? To come to this? Your own not having faith in themselves anymore? Oh, he felt like killing the whole damn world.

That story lets you know one of the first things about the way Hispanics view the dominant culture — that "they" are better than us. They — the white Americanos — are richer, whiter, smarter, holier, luckier, and better than Hispanics. And can one be blamed for thinking and feeling this way when life appears to continually deal you a rotten hand? An example of this is how even higher education does not necessarily open more doors for Hispanics. In another book, *Empowering Hispanic Families: Critical Issues for the 90s,* one of the authors quotes research that shows that the economic gap between white non-Hispanic and Mexican American workers widens with increased levels of education. In other words, years of college may result in diminishing returns for Hispanic professionals. Thus, the social structure rewards Hispanic initiative in the blue-collar job market, but entrance into the white-collar domain may be viewed as trespassing.

I remember when I graduated from high school in 1961, how amazed my family was that the only job I could find in my profession paid the same wage they were getting in the factories!

I graduated in June; I had been accepted into my religious community and I was joining in September. But I needed to work in the summer because in those days, we had to bring in a dowry and we didn't have one. I belonged to a family in New York that lived on welfare, so I was trying to get a job in the profession I trained for, which was the fashion industry. I thought I was going to be a fashion designer, until the Lord rerouted me.

But I wanted to work at least that summer in something that had to do with the fashion trade. I finally got a job in a pretty exclusive women's dress shop — in the back, altering dresses. I came home all proud that I had gotten a job. And my family said, "What are they going to pay you?" Those were the days of $1 an hour, and I said, "I'm going to get $40 a week." It sounded like a fortune to me and my family looked at me and laughed. They all worked in factories, where minimum wage was the law, so they all got $40 a week also, but they only had third-grade educations.

My family comes from the mountainous part of Puerto Rico, where you're lucky if there was a little school that went up to third grade. To go any higher, you had to go into the town and my mother's family couldn't do that. So they learned to read and write at only a third-grade level. They said to me, "What did you go to high school for? You went through all this education and you end up getting paid no more than we do?"

Is it any wonder that we conclude that the other race is better than ours?

To better understand these concepts, look at Table 1. These lists were compiled by Sister Maria de la Cruz Aymes in workshops with Hispanics. She asks workshop members to list the 10 most important values for themselves. Then they are asked to list the American hierarchy of values, as they see them.

Table 1

Hierarchy of Hispanic Values (as perceived by Hispanics)	Hierarchy of American Values (as perceived by Hispanics)
1. Family	1. Money
2. Hospitality	2. Materialism
3. "Carino"	3. Individualism
4. Religiosity	4. Work
5. Celebrations	5. Education
6. Community	6. Technology
7. Education	7. Organization
8. School	8. Punctuality
9. Work	9. Family
10. Money	10. Religion

This is the way it comes out almost invariably with very few changes. For Hispanics, family is always first. Hospitality is somewhere near there. Religiosity is fourth, but sometimes it's second. Number 3, "carino," means affection, caring, warmth, life, and love. Then, celebrations, community, education, and school.

It may surprise you to find education and school on the same list. But education is not necessarily a form of schooling for the Hispanic. Anyone can be educated in the Spanish cultures, even the person who can't read. An educated person is someone who knows how to treat you as a human being. So the first thing the man who lives off in the hills says when he sees you is, "Come into my house and have a cup of coffee or water." He is a man who is educated. The man who has three Ph.Ds but is a bore is an uneducated person. School is formal education.

In the second list, Hispanics perceive that Americans rank money as the most important thing, followed by materialism, individualism, work, education (education here means school) technology, organization, punctuality, family, and religion.

Notice the differences in the lists? Family is first to Hispanics. Money is last on the list. This doesn't mean that money is not important to Hispanics — we know it's important and work very hard to get it — but if you ask them for 10 values, money ends up last. Where do they perceive money belongs in the American culture? First. So you see right away a big difference between these two worlds, a virtual collision between these two worlds.

One of the results of this clash of values is that it causes tremendous confusion in determining identity. This is especially true for youth. One grows up at home with one set of values and is given, or taught, a completely different set in society at large. And one of the difficulties is that no one tells us that these values are clashing. That it isn't, in reality, a case of better or worse but simply a case of different or other. In my experience, neither the dominant culture nor my own Hispanic culture was able to explain to me that I am caught between two cultures — one that has traditional values and one that is based on the values of a technological society. And what works in one does not necessarily work in the other.

Table 2

Task-Oriented Culture	Family-Oriented Culture
1. Confrontation	1. Reticence, indirection
2. Competition and independence	2. Support
3. Individualism	3. Affiliation to group (family)
4. Fair play and cooperation	4. Find consensus difficult
5. Superficiality in relationships	5. Intimacy
6. Equality through achievement	6. Class ranking and status
7. Informality	7. Formality
8. Comfort	8. Style
9. Need to be liked	9. Need to be loved
10. Materialism	10. Spirituality
11. Future-orientation	11. Present- / past-orientation
12. "I" - ism	12. "We" - ism
13. Self-motivation	13. Group motivation
14. Planning, perfect organization	14. Improvisation
15. Serious, intense	15. Happy-go-lucky (relaxed)
16. Celebration of effort	16. Celebration of life

Table 2 provides a sense of otherness of the two cultures our youth are growing up in. These lists are no longer how Hispanics view the dominant culture but rather, based on sociological and anthropological studies, how cultures that are family-oriented (Hispanic, Asian, Native American) differ from cultures that are task-oriented (American).

Task-oriented cultures tend to be confrontative; family-oriented cultures tend to be reticent and indirect. Confrontation doesn't mean being nasty and always attacking people; it just means these cultures are very direct, especially in their communications. I call a person and I get right to the point because my time is important; I don't have much of it and the telephone costs money. The Hispanic culture, a family-oriented culture, communicates at a less-hurried pace.

This story should illustrate my point. There are a number of Hispanic seminarians where I work. Most came to the United States as poor immigrants. I told the seminarians that when I'm home and I'm not using my car, they are welcome to use it. One day, a seminarian named Solomé came into my office. From the moment he walks in, I know he wants to use my car. But he stands there and says, "Mother Veronica, how are you?"

"I'm fine," I answered.

He says, "You look very busy."

"Yes, I am busy."

"What is it that you are doing?"

"Well, I am doing a report."

"Madre, how is your mother?"

"My mother is fine."

I'm going insane because I have work to do and I want him to say, "Sister, may I borrow your car?" Ten minutes later, Solomé says, "May I borrow your car, Madre?"

"Yes, Solomé."

If I asked Solomé to just walk in and say, "Sister, do you need the car? May I borrow it?", I would cause such confusion with this young man, because down in his genes, this is the rudest way of

84

behaving, and he would leave thinking, "What did I do to offend her?"

So you see that the whole way of communicating is different.

Americans communicate very directly; Hispanics communicate very circularly. If we don't know that, we get into all kinds of misunderstandings.

Now let's look at another area where the American and Hispanic cultures differ. As you know, different cultures learn differently. In the United States, independence is highly valued. Privacy is highly valued. In other cultures, the community is valued, and that is how you learn. A Christian brother I know had spent almost 17 years in Peru. When he first went down there, he gave his students a test. The students all sat together and began to share the answers. He went insane. He said, "This is cheating, this is lying, this is against the Eighth Commandment." Then he went and talked to the headmaster of the school. The headmaster sat him down and said, "Brother, do you think perhaps the values and the way you learned in your country might be different than the way we learn here? You see, the value for us is not who gets the highest grade all by himself. The value for us is that the community should pass that test, everyone in the community. So the bright ones must help the less bright one and give him his answers."

I grew up in New York, so I'm one of the schizophrenic two-cultures-in-one-skin people. I went to Catholic elementary school and I got to the eighth grade, the adolescent time of religious awakening. Test time would come, and my friends would all ask, "Veronica, what's the answer to this?" When I helped them, I had to go to confession and I was getting a little tired of confessing that I had cheated. I didn't know what to do, so like a good daughter I went to my mother. "Mom, what do you think about cheating in tests?" I asked her.

"I would die from embarrassment if anyone ever said to me that you cheated in a test," she said.

I said to her, "Well, what do I do when my friends ask me for answers?"

"Oh, that's all right, you can help them," she said. "But I don't want you cheating." To my mother, it was not cheating; it was helping.

So if you learn this way — if you learn in community — then you don't learn just by reading books, and you don't learn just by yourself. Educational methods used in the United States are not necessarily the most productive.

I'm not saying that you have to change it to fit all of these different peoples. But we do have to become aware that different peoples' cultures have different styles. And if we want to teach effectively, we somehow have to find a middle ground somewhere.

Few people I know would disagree that family and spirituality are two of the greatest gifts Hispanics bring to this country. And these two, family and religion, are so closely intertwined that they are almost the same thing. In all the research done on Hispanics, the family emerges as the most important support network available to Hispanics, and that thought must be recognized and supported by the helping profession. In order to use this value effectively with youth, one has to understand the different way we experience family.

As you know, ours is an extended sense of family. I joined the convent in 1961, in the years when we had all these rules of cloister and people could only come see us once a month. I joined in September. In October my family came for their first monthly visit. Five or six cars pulled up at the front door of the Mother House and at least 10 to 15 people fell out of each car. This one little nun who was near me looked at them and said, "Who are all these people?" I said, "They're my family." And she said, "All of them?" All the aunts, all the cousins. No one had a car, so the neighbor who had the car got enlisted. Family is all of that for us.

The importance of the extended family for at-risk youth was one of the conclusions reached as a result of research done on Puerto Rican drug addicts by the New York Jesuit and sociologist, Father Joseph Fitzpatrick. One hypothesis he hoped to prove in this research was that youth whose families were intact — that is, had both a father and a mother — had less tendency to become addicted to drugs than youth who came from what we call "broken homes." What the research found was that youth who knew that a godmother, an aunt, an uncle, cousins, or family friends who are family were watching when mother wasn't, and who received support not only from their family but also from the rest of the extended family, were less likely to succumb to drug addiction. And if they did, they were the ones who were able to recover.

Understanding the Hispanic sense of family is more than just understanding the extendedness of Hispanic families. In his book, *Pastoral Counseling Across Cultures*, David Augsburger points out that in technological cultures there tends to be an interpersonal contract view of the family as a "roof organization." For example, all people who speak Spanish — whether they are from Puerto Rican, Cuban, Guatemalan, etc., culture — are labeled "Hispanic."

The traditional cultures of the world, however, see the family as a "root organism," with a basic foundational oneness that persons emerge from into an individuated consciousness at widely varied life stages. One must be careful here. We can easily fall into the trap of thinking that we can use this value of family and never realize that the very concept of family in our two cultures is different. For one, it's an organization; for the other, it's an organism.

Hispanics are not the only ones who give such an exalted place to family. I have said that Italians are far more Latino than they are Anglo. I know that whatever I say about family resonates in the souls of those of you who have Italian roots. And in case anyone doubts me, consider this quote from a book written by a good Italian writer — *The Madonna of 115th Street: Faith and Community in Italian Harlem, 1880-1950*, by Robert Orsi. Quoting Italians he interviewed, Orsi writes: "The home is the religion of Italian Americans....We are taught two things, religion, and we are taught family life."

Earlier in the book, he writes: "It is not far from the truth to say that for many Italians, whatever religion they possess is narrowed within the walls of the home, for the home of the Italian is essentially religious."

This also is true for Hispanics. A few stories from *Rain of Gold* should convince you of this. It also will give you a sense of Hispanic popular religiosity. I entitled this article "Sometimes Even God Needs Help" for a number of reasons. One reason is that attitude, that familiarity with God, that daring to think that we might be able to help God, that maybe God needs a push from us, that at-homeness with God, are qualities of Hispanic popular religiosity.

As I mentioned earlier, the family of the author of *Rain of Gold* had migrated up from Mexico and in the process, many members of the family had been lost. At one point in the story, the paternal grandmother of the author is feeling the pain of having lost so many children; of 17, she can count only two or three. She has the custom of going to church every day and has a heart-to-heart talk with the Blessed Virgin Mary. One day she comes out of church determined to go to Chicago because Mary has told her that one of her few remaining sons is there. Her daughter naturally is upset. This is an old, frail woman who does not speak English. So the daughter calls on her brother, the mother's youngest, to talk some sense into their mother. The mother responds to the son by saying:

"Don't listen to her; I know what I'm doing. You see, I went to church the other day, and I spoke to the Virgin Mary, woman to woman, telling her of my grief at having lost so many sons, and then I had this vision." (There is a sense here that Mary, who had lost her Son on the cross, understands a mother's pain at losing her children.)

So she proceeds to explain how Mary informed her that her son was in Chicago. In the process, she keeps talking about Jesus, and so her son asks her, "Mother I thought you were talking to Mary."

"Oh, I was," she said. "But you know how her son is always putting his nose into everything."

There is that certain familiarity with God. Family is important enough to bring in the highest of our heavenly hierarchy, and religion is what holds together and heals the family.

As the story continues, the mother is determined to go to Chicago. Her son tries to reason with her, telling her that she has no idea where Chicago is.

"Did I know where Guadalajara was when I was sent to save Jose from his execution?" she answers. "Did we know where the United States was when we left the mountains? No, a person never needs to know where to go. What is needed is the conviction, here inside your soul, that you will overcome whatever it takes to get there."

Conviction, sense of mission, a reason for being — these all come from the strong sense of family.

In another part of the story, the mother is giving her son some advice that really means that Juan would have to lie. The son challenges her by asking her how she would feel if he lied to her. She responds:

"Me? Well, I want the truth of course. But my world isn't based on right or wrong, mi hijito. It's based on love and doing whatever a mother needs to get done to survive. Just like God in the heavens and His responsibilities of the universe, I'd lie ten thousand times a day to help my family."

Family is the highest value in the Hispanic hierarchy and religion is right up there with it.

At another point of the story, the son, completely exasperated, asks his mother, "Mom, this is incredible. Where did you learn this?"

She responds: "Why, in the outhouse of course. (She would get up in the morning, take her Bible, her little cigar, and a little shot of the bootleg whiskey her son would make, and head out to the outhouse and sit with the Bible in her lap.) What in God's name do you think the Virgin and I talk about all these mornings that I spend with her? We speak about the Word of God, mi hijito, and not as if it happened years ago, but as it is happening now, here, today with us."

The importance of this sense of family and spirituality for our youth cannot be exaggerated. It lets them know who they are and corrects the erroneous self-image that is often the result of being a member of a so-called "minority culture." It gives our young people a sense of origin, roots, a past, a memory. Orsi states the importance of this very well in his book:

89

"Personal integrity and stability depend on the ability to remember. Memory locates the individual in a community: Individuals share memories with various groups — family, neighborhood, city and so on — and this communion of memory is the foundation of their membership in these groups. Memory is also that which binds men and women together in their most intimate relations with their families. Older members of the family share their recollections, which are often part of a corporate memory they too had once been taught, with their younger kin, who in this way are invited and integrated into the generations. Memory finally helps share personal identities: Men and women discover who they are in their memory."

That discovering of who we are, in my opinion, is one of the contributions Hispanics make to the broader culture. We are a constant reminder to everyone that we all began somewhere. That all of us, if we but take the time to look, will find roots intricate and beyond unraveling, immensely rich in history, a history filled with grace. This process of finding out who we are, of finding our roots, is for all of us the essence of our religiosity.

In *Pastoral Counseling Across Cultures*, Augsburger writes: "There is no such thing as theology immune from cultural and historical influences. Theology is culturally and historically not neutral. A neutral theology is in fact a homeless theology. It does not belong anywhere. Thus theology really begins in earnest when it identifies its home and discovers its belonging.

"We say theology is the work of interpreting God's presence and work with all humanity. Thus all persons must root their theologies firmly in their own culture, while expanding that theology's vision and perspective."

A few weeks ago I did a workshop in Joliet and I started off by asking them questions: "Who are your people? Why did they come to the United States? How did they practice their religiosity? What aspect did you keep, what did you let go of and why?" It was a small room, so while they were doing that part of the dynamic I could hear them. And I heard this lady, in one of the most sad-feeling voices I've ever heard, say, "I can't do this. I don't know my roots."

Her family was fourth-, fifth-, sixth-, seventh-generation Americans. They have intermarried here and there and along the way they had become "American." And so she knew there was something Scottish back there; maybe something German. But she couldn't do it. And it was such a sadness to her that she couldn't do it.

Unlike many other immigrants who came to this country, Hispanics hold their countries of origin so close that the constant movement back and forth to the homeland continues to solidify and revitalize their culture and language in the United States. So we are forever trying to remember and to figure out who we are. And while doing this, we jog your memories, whether or not you want us to! This is why it is so essential for Hispanic young people to know who they are. Their Hispanic culture is proving to be resistant to the fires of the melting pot and unlike other immigrants, they still have strong cultural and linguistic, and thus emotional, bonds that transcend geographical and political boundaries.

In Mexico, outside of the city of Cuernavaca, there is a place similar to Boys Town. It was founded by an American priest, a Franciscan who had little boys who were stealing from the collection box. When the police came, the Franciscan said, "Leave them with me; they were only stealing because they were hungry."

Within two weeks, he had 12 more boys and the police kept bringing children to him. Today, there are about 1,000 boys and girls in this one place in Mexico. From third grade on, they clean, make their own beds, wash their own clothes, grow the corn to make the tortillas, and do their own cooking. For a population of 1,000, they have maybe 100 adults. They are self-sufficient and responsible, and the children are never put up for adoption. When a child comes, this place becomes his or her family.

I visited them last year. I never saw a happier group of kids; I didn't think it was possible to be a child in an institution and be happy. There was no anger, no bitterness at life, no "Look at what life has done to me. Why can't I be home with my own mother and father?" This is their family.

Because of the Hispanic sense of family extendedness, any

91

group that takes a person in and values that person as an individual can become family. If you could succeed in getting kids to tap into that very high value of family, you just might save a few youth.

It is very difficult for me to speak about negative aspects of Hispanic culture. Not because I am not aware that there is as much sin in Hispanic culture as there is in all other cultures, but because I have begun to wonder: Are these things that we call negatives really negatives or is it simply that they don't work here?

I keep telling my Hispanic seminarians that they are in this country and they have to learn what the values and realities are in this country. I say to them, "You know you keep trying to play American football with Latin American soccer rules and it doesn't work." When you transplant the two values I gave you — family and religiosity — in American culture in the United States, it doesn't work.

Family is a very strong value to us, but we know that Hispanic families have been broken all over the place. If child-care facilities have Hispanic children, it's because their grandmother or their aunt or somebody did not take them to finish the growing-up process. Strong value though it is, it does not necessarily withstand the assets of the post-modern culture that our United States reality is in. And the values that keep us together do not necessarily work here.

I'll give you an example. In Chicago there is a young Mexican American man who finished high school. I think he was born in the United States. He was intelligent enough and talented enough to be given a scholarship to Harvard. Completely free, all expenses paid. His father said, "You're not going." This would be shocking to someone who has good American values of education and knows how expensive education is. Here, it was coming free to this young man. Imagine the doors that would open for him when he said, "I graduated from Harvard." All those values are there.

But what was the value of the father? "You're too far from the family. I don't want you that far; you have to stay close to us." The young man did not go to Harvard. Now, in the father's country, maybe that works. In the United States, we look at it from our cultural viewpoint and seriously question whether something good was done for that young man.

Even popular religiosity doesn't work too well in the United States. One of the things that makes religiosity popular is that it permeates every level of existence. In popular religiosity, the sacred and the profane are not separated. Orsi speaks of Italian popular religiosity in New York this way: "The world of the sacred was not entered only, or even mainly in churches; it was encountered and celebrated through family life, hospitality, and friendship, as well as in the daily trials of the people."

In the United States, from its very foundations, we have separated the sacred and the profane. Our Constitution is based on separation of church and state. Religion is to stay within our individual temples and God is not supposed to enter into the other spheres of our lives. Is it any wonder that the way we practice religion in this country does not feed people who come from cultures that are in themselves religious?

So there are negatives, and I will mention a very important one. But I want us to be aware that the negativity may be much more in our perception than in the reality. In fact, research by a man named Calzado Buriel has shown how investigators have often portrayed Mexican Americans as the victims of their own culture. Poverty and an alarming high school dropout rate — all problems great and small — traditionally have been laid on the doorstep of a damaged (and damaging) parent culture. Such explanations, of course, conveniently absolve mainstream America of blame. Buriel also cites less well-known research that supports his thesis that traditional Mexican American values promote achievement instead of failure.

One of the negatives in Hispanic cultures is our color consciousness. Remember the first story from *Rain of Gold*, the one where Juan is working with his two nephews and the older of the two, Jose, is asking about the father he never got to know? As Juan is telling him how good his father was, he says:

"I was just about your age when he and Luisa got married, and he showed me a lot of love. I stayed with them and he put me on his lap, calling me his amo. I loved him. He never abused me like my own father did."

"You mean that your own father was bad to you?" asked the boy.

Juan had to laugh. "Hell, my father treated the dogs better than me. He only had eyes for my brother Domingo, who was blue-eyed like himself."

"You mean, our Papagrande wouldn't have liked us either," said Jose, turning to his brother Pedro, "because we got dark eyes?"

Juan was sorry that he had started the whole thing, but he wasn't going to lie to his nephews now. "Maybe not," he said. "There's a lot of prejudice in Mexico, too, you know."

As Juan says, there's a lot of prejudice in our own countries, too. However, it is different and we deal with it better in our countries than we do in the United States. When we come to the United States, this prejudice that we already have gets compounded by America's own obsession with color.

Hispanics were taught that whites were more beautiful than brown or black from the very arrival of the Spaniards. Hispanic color racism is not quite the same as racism in the United States, but it is real and its consequences can and have been documented. The following quote comes from the chapter, "Phenotyping, Acculturation, and Biracial Assimilation of Mexican Americans" in the book, *Empowering Hispanic Families*.

"Research has shown that the more dark and Indian in appearance they were, the more Mexican Americans felt disliked, ignored, and uncared for, which is consistent with darker Chicanos reporting more discrimination."

But while it is true that more discrimination may happen in the United States, it also is true that the self-dislike is already there even before the darker Mexican or Hispano comes to this country. We are forever saying, "Isn't she pretty? She looks like an Italian." Or, "Isn't she lovely? She looks like she's Jewish. Oh, isn't that wonderful?" The boast in many a Puerto Rican family is, "I have people in my family who have green eyes." This is what we hear.

Unfortunately, we are of a race that the sun stays with very nicely without first torturing us. And yet you find people not going into the sun because they don't want to be any darker than they already are. A recent study on racial phenotypes reported that education and income levels of Chicano subjects increased significantly according to the lightness of their skin color and the extent to which their appearance seemed European.

Phenotyping is a crucial factor in influencing the process of allocating more social and economic opportunities to individuals who most resemble racially the members of the dominant group.

Accordingly, the wide variation in skin coloration of Hispanic children causes them to experience differing stress and to develop differing response patterns as they and their families strive to balance sociocultural continuity with accommodation to America's system of racial stratification.

And it doesn't help that the way we handle this in our countries of origin is different from the way it is in the United States. Cultural patterns in the Americas provide for more open forms of conviviality and permit a wider range of phenotypical differences to exist in families while allowing their cultural identity to remain firm. When Hispanics emigrate to the United States, they expect to encounter a similar pattern of race relations. They expect high mobility. But "Hispanics in general, and Puerto Ricans in particular do not understand race as do most people in the United States" (Massey & Denton, 1989), nor do they understand how a biracial system will affect the cultural identity and ethnic affiliation of their children.

How do we turn this around? How do we address these negatives as challenges to grow in our work of fostering spiritual growth among at-risk youth?

Perhaps the greatest negative in Hispanic cultures is the same negative found in all cultures: We are forever expecting others to be just like we are and when they are not, we immediately conclude there is something wrong with them! For me, the most effective thing we can do to turn any negative into a positive that will challenge others to grow is to facilitate an understanding of what is happening. That is, help young people to know, study, discover, and be curious about where they came from; in other words, know, really know, who they are. Then help them cross over and know who the others are. If I can come to the realization that while I am no better than others and I am certainly no worse, then perhaps I will not only insist on my right to be who I am but also will defend the right of others to be "other" than I am.

However, how effectively I facilitate this process of discovering depends on how well I know myself. How aware are we that all of us are encased in our own cultural straight jackets and that this affects all that we do?

We have a tendency in the United States to say that there is no such thing as American culture. But any country, any society that has existed as long as ours has a culture. We are encased in that cultural straight jacket and we look at the world through the lenses of that culture.

Our young Hispanics need to develop the ability to cross over to the American culture without losing their own. But if we haven't developed that ability ourselves, we will not be able to help them. David Augsburger says crossing over to another culture with openness and reverence and then coming back is the spiritual adventure of our time. He also says that awareness of one's own culture can free one to disconnect identity from cultural externals and to live on the boundary, crossing over and coming back with increasing freedom.

In closing, I want to share this story from the Gospel of Matthew, 15:24-30. The credit for this interpretation goes to Jack Shea ("The Story of the Cyrophenician Women"). It is an example of what has been discussed and will explain my other reason for choosing the title "Sometimes Even God Needs Help."

Shea says this is one of the boldest stories in the Bible. It is the only one in which Jesus changes his mind. Along with the story are

96

some questions and comments about what the story means.

"Then Jesus left that place and we drew along the border of Tyre and Sidon."

What does it mean to walk along borders? What were the borders that separated people at the time of Jesus? There were three main ones: Female/Male, Jew/Gentile, Master/Slave. This is a Jew/Gentile border. This is an ethnic story. This is the story of one border walker meeting another border walker.

"Behold, a Canaanite woman from those borders, coming forth, cried out to him, 'Lord, Son of David, have mercy on me! My daughter is terribly troubled by a demon.'" (You see, she too had an at-risk child.)

What is the Canaanite woman like? Jesus withdrew, but she approaches very aggressively. She is screaming and crying out, and who is she? The word "Behold" lets you know. In Scripture, "Behold" announces the one who brings the Word of God, the message of God. Behold is used for John the Baptist; John the Baptist uses "behold" for Jesus. In this story, "behold" is for the woman.

This woman knows who Jesus is — Lord, the Savior, the Son of David, a Jew. She is very assertive. She knows the truth. She knows Jesus is a Jew, but a Jew meant for everyone.

In a way, she is the paradigm of a perfect believer. She knows who He is, she knows what He can do, and she wants it for someone other than herself.

Jesus gives her no word of response and the apostles misinterpret His silence. They think He's uncomfortable and embarrassed. Here's this woman making a scene, yelling and screaming, and they are like many a follower who tries to read the mind of the leader and then say what they think He wants them to say. And so they say to Him, "Get rid of her, she keeps shouting after us."

But they got it wrong. Jesus starts thinking out loud and says to them, "No, that's not what is bothering me about her. My mission is only to the lost sheep of the house of Israel."

And the key word here is "house." Who gets into the house? It is those who are in the house who eat. Jesus is thinking out loud, trying to sort out what His mission is. His problem is that He has wrapped His mission around one ethnic group — the Jews. The woman hears this and coming forward, does Him homage with the plea, "Help me Lord." Notice she dropped "the Son of David." If being a Jew was the problem to Him, she would let it go. But she still reminds Him, "You are Lord," which in their culture means, "Giver of Mercy."

But He answers, "It is not right to take the food of the sons and daughters and throw it to the dogs."

"Yes, Lord," she says. "But even dogs eat the leavings that fall from their masters' tables."

What is happening here? It could very well be a reference to the fact that Jews and Gentiles treated their dogs differently. The Jews kept their dogs outside the house; Gentiles let their dogs inside. Jesus is saying, "If I help her, I have to go out of the house, out of my Jewish identity, in order to feed her."

The woman says, "No, you don't have to go out of the house. I am already inside. I am underneath the table where the scraps will reach me. You don't have to leave your identity to help me."

So far, Jesus has not really addressed her. Now He does.

"Oh woman, you have great faith, let it be done to you as you desire."

By using the title "Woman," Jesus gives her great praise. The only other time Jesus uses the title is for Mary. And the words, "Let it be done," the fiat, "Let it be done to you as you desire." She has told Him the will of God. It was the will of God that He be a Jew but a Jew that is meant for everyone. She has reminded Him of his universal call, of His real identity. But calling Him to be more than a Jew, she frees Him to truly be a Jew.

"That very moment, the daughter got better."

Why is the cure instantaneous? Jesus had been stuck seeing His mission only in relation to the Jews. When this woman, who in a way is the presence of God for Him, helps to unblock Him, the floodgates open and mercy pours out and the daughter is healed at that very moment. Two border walkers meet and God's healing presence is felt.

When in your work you seem to be getting nowhere — neither crossing over too successfully yourself nor succeeding at getting others to cross — remember that sometimes, even God needs help.

SR. VERONICA MENDEZ, RCD, is director of the Hispanic Ministry Program at Mundelein Seminary in Mundelein, Illinois. She has served as a director of religious education and a parish minister in South Carolina, Florida, and New York City. She presently is a member of the Executive Committee of CORHIM (Conference of Religion for Hispanic Ministry) and was on the advisory board for the Fund for Theological Education: Hispanic Summer Seminar. Her essay in this volume was first presented at the 1993 symposium, "Fostering Spiritual Growth Among At-Risk Youth: Multicultural Perspectives."

REFERENCES

Augsburger, D.W. (1986). **Pastoral counseling across cultures: A theology of culture, a theology of presence, a theology of counseling.** Philadelphia: The Westminster Press.

Fitzpatrick, J.P. (1971). **Puerto Rican Americans: The meaning of migration to the mainland.** Englewood Cliffs, NJ: Prentice Hall.

Fitzpatrick, J.P & Gould, R.E. (1970). **Mental illness among Puerto Ricans in New York: Cultural condition or intercultural misunderstanding?** New York: Fordham University.

Fitzpatrick, J.P. (1959). **Delinquency and the Puerto Ricans.** New York: Migration Division, Department of Labor.

Massey, D.S., & Denton, N.A. (1989). **Hypersegregation in U.S. metropolitan areas: Black and Hispanic segregation along five dimensions.** Chicago: Population Association of America.

Mendez, V. (1990). **MTS theses on formation of Hispanic women.** Berkeley.

Orsi, R. (1985). **Madonna of 115th street: Faith and community in Italian Harlem, 1880-1950.** New Haven, CT: Yale University Press.

Sotomayor, M. (1991). **Empowering Hispanic families: Critical issues for the '90s.** Milwaukee: Family Services of America.

Villasenor, V. (1992). **Rain of Gold.** Houston: Arte Publico Press.

CHAPTER SIX

Approaches to Resiliency: An African-Centered Perspective

DR. NSENGA WARFIELD-COPPOCK

There is a saying, "If we don't change directions, we may end up where we're heading." A lot of people have recognized this need to change and they offer new directions for our young people. I am grateful to be able to share my views on this pressing challenge to our country's future.

I greet you in the words of our African brothers and sisters in the language of Kiswahili — "Jambo." I greet you in the words of our Nigerian ancestor, the language of the Yoruba people, "Alafia." "Wo ho te sen" is the way our Ghanaian brothers and sisters may greet you in the language of Twi; "Na-Nga-Def" is the language of the Wolof people of Senegal. "Hotep" means "Peace" and is a greeting from our most ancient civilization and ancestors, Khemet-Land of the Blacks, otherwise called Egypt.

I greet you in the languages of our land of origin because I believe as the ancient proverb says: *To go back to tradition is the first step forward.*

I'd like to tell you about a symbol from the Akan people of West Africa. It is the Sankafo bird. This bird has a very long neck and it stretches back to its tail. This symbolizes learning from the past. In this article, I'm going to give you some of our past and traditional concepts to see how they can assist us in the challenges of today's world and with today's youth.

101

I had an opportunity about three years ago to take my two daughters, who were then 10 and 14, to Dakar, Senegal in West Africa. I was at a turning point, a situation where I was thinking about leaving one job and moving to do something different. So, it was a good place to go and just kind of reflect. We went with a number of people from Senegal. We didn't speak Wolof and I don't speak French so it was a good thing that we had other people with us to communicate.

One of the things we did when we traveled to Senegal was to visit the island of Goreé, known as the island where Africans were held prior to being shipped all over the world as slaves. There is one house they call the slave house and it has been turned into a museum. As you enter this house, you go in and on the other side of the house there is an exit. The exit is to the ocean and they call it the Door of No Return, because once Africans moved through that door they did not come back. They say that on the island of Goreé the water ran red because Africans would jump overboard and be eaten by sharks rather than be enslaved.

We also learned an interesting story about a huge tree. I have a friend who is from there and is a history buff, and he has been doing research on Dakar and Goreé. He told me that this was the baobab tree. The baobab tree is not a particularly good-looking tree — it is kind of scruffy and not real tall. It is low to the earth, but it is very solid and its foundation and roots are very deep. He said you never hear of this type of tree being uprooted. Apparently, the French who colonized the Senegalese area measured these trees in the 1750s and some were 100 to 200 feet in circumference. My friend told me that the French came back and measured the same trees about 50 years later and found that they had grown one foot in circumference in that 50-year period. Can you imagine how old these trees are now? So I asked him some more about these trees. He said the people believed that their ancestors reside in the tree. If a person wanted some inspiration or wanted to acquire some knowledge from the past, one could go sit at the base of this tree. He told me that the older men of the community often would just sit at the base of this tree all day, and the women couldn't pull them away so they had to take their lunch to them.

This tree became a symbol for the business I started right after coming back from Dakar. I did so because it is my hope that by taking ancestral knowledge — knowledge from the past — and applying it to contemporary problems and challenges that we will in fact be able to solve some of these problems. This is what is being done when we apply the concept of the rites of passage.

I would like to tell you about the ritual of Libation. Libation is like a prayer that is used by Africans and African Americans to acknowledge the importance of our ancestors. It is a ritual that is becoming increasingly common in African American communities. For example, in a movie called *Cooley High*, there was a part where three or four young men skipped school and got a bottle of wine to share among themselves. The first young man to open the bottle poured a little on the ground and said, "This is for the brothers who aren't here." They were offering a Libation for those who have passed on. This was an informal Libation demonstrated in the popular media.

The Libation is like a prayer which offers a liquid symbolically to ancestors. It is a communal ritual which invites you to come and drink.

The following is an example of a Libation. If you were to come to my house, I would offer you something to drink and say a prayer. I would expect you to say "Ashe" after each line of my prayer. Ashe simply means "I agree" in a Nigerian language — Yebo (in Zulu).

RITUAL:

We call on the ancestors to come and join us here today. (Ashe)
We ask that you be with us as we contemplate the issues of our
  high-risk young people. (Ashe)
We ask that you come and join us that you bring wisdom and
  knowledge that we need to help these young people. (Ashe)
I call on Martin Luther King, Jr. (Ashe)

103

I call on Sojourner Truth. (Ashe)
I call on Marcus Garvey. (Ashe)
I call on Malcolm X. (Ashe)
I call on Thurgood Marshall. (Ashe)
We ask that you be with us, that you help us, that you give us
    part of your wisdom and knowledge, and help us to solve
    the problems of the young people in our communities today.
    (Ashe)

That particular ritual is one that we use very often in development of a rite of passage program. I had the opportunity to consult with a rite of passage program developed in the Washington, D.C., area for teen mothers. These girls were in the Health and Human Services system because of child abuse and neglect or sexual abuse. All of the girls were between the ages of 14 and 19 and each had between one and four children. These girls, obviously, came with a lot of problems. It was felt that a rite to passage to womanhood and parenthood at the same time would assist them not only in their own growth and development, but also in breaking the cycle of abuse.

We instituted this particular ritual with them. I was at the first orientation with these 11 girls. The girls were not interested. You know how teenagers can be; they laid around and acted like they didn't want to be bothered with anything. But as the program got going, they started arguing about who was going to pour the Libation! They actually got into the concept of Libation and family and who their family ancestors were. It became a very positive experience for them.

A second ritual is Elder Permission. I believe it is important to return our elders to their eldership status so that they may share their wisdom from the past with us. Elder Permission simply means that we treat our elders with respect and look to them for advice. They lived in a past of safer times with less violence, less drug use and abuse, fewer disordered families, and less abuse of children. We, as they do, should find all of these things intolerable.

Young people need to understand the relationship of elders in their families and in their community. In traditional African communities and most communities of color, the elders were highly revered and respected. In traditional African society, of course, there were councils of elders. So, in this particular program I worked with, The Teen Mothers program, we set up a council of elders — a group of women who became guides and confidantes for the teenage girls. Often these girls had not had a real positive relationship or an opportunity to relate to an older woman in their family or in the community. It became a very positive experience for the girls.

Both the Libation and Elder Permission are important because they put things into a proper perspective. There is a hierarchy; we have God, we have the ancestors, the elders, and then the rest of us — parents and children. Traditionally, this is how the communities were set up, built, and functioned. A lot of that has broken down. It has broken down because being young is so highly revered now. Everybody wants to look young and avoid getting old.

I was the keynote speaker at a conference in Hampton, Virginia. (They already had elders in their community.) The man who introduced everyone at the conference got up after the Libation and asked Elder Reed if he could have permission to continue. Elder Reed stood up and started asking him questions. He said, "Well, is everything in order?" The man assured Elder Reed that it was and answered all of his questions. Elder Reed then said, "Fine. Go ahead." I had never seen that before. Usually it is just a kind of perfunctory interaction. It was interesting to see that kind of interplay. It was obvious that the elders played an important part in that community and had been working there for some time.

I did some analysis of the topic of fostering spiritual growth among at-risk youth. In my education and training over the years, I have noted a tendency for Western science to separate topics and subject matter into smaller pieces as well as to create dichotomies. Much of the theory and thinking coming out of Western psychology is based on the thinking of 17th century philosopher, Rene Descartes, which attempted to separate the mind and body. The

105

Cartesian dualism persists in the ways that we frame problems and their solutions as well. When I thought about the topic of fostering spiritual growth, I decided to reject separatist notions and remain holistic.

An African-centered perspective simply means that we are looking at the world through an African eye. I would like to discuss how the African perspective has assisted our communities in changing our high-risk youth into successful, competent, and cultural young people.

I would like to discuss what has been called Afrocentric theory. Defined, Afrocentricity means "the study of African phenomenon from the position of African people in the world as subject, rather than object." In other words, central to African history and to world history.

There is some belief that the Afrocentric orientation or model being introduced into program development does not have its basis in theory. This is not true. I have studied Western philosophy and theory as well as African philosophy and theory. The models that are currently discussed by theorists and scholars such as Wade Nobles, Molefi Asante, Mbiti, Karenga, Asa Hilliard, Osei, and many others are indeed based in solid theory.

I studied African philosophy as well as European philosophy. I learned African person-oriented family and kinship models as well as European and Asian familial and relational styles. I considered the European models of organizations as well as the history of African American organizations. What I found (like many others before and since me) were some striking differences. These differences began to logically explain the things that had been sitting dormant in my thinking patterns.

I am an Afrocentric psychologist. You may ask why. I made that choice when all that was required of me by the educational system was that I learn the traditional European models. I studied the additional cultural models because if you have a standard square hole, a round peg will not fit. The models of traditional psychology did not fit the form of African American behavior and thinking.

There is a story that a friend of mine uses to illustrate this point: There are dogs raised specifically to be sheep dogs. That is, they are raised to take care of sheep that wander aimlessly if not watched. After the puppy is born, it is taken from its mother and placed in the care of a mother sheep. The ewe nurses and nurtures the dog into adulthood. The dog learns to act like a sheep in many ways. The end result is that the dog will look out for the sheep without worry from the owner that the dog will harm or attack them in any way. The question: Is it a sheep or is it a dog?

The same question is asked of an African person who is raised in the way of the European — in his schools, churches, political, and economic system: Is she or he an African or a European? If the African person is then taught the ways of her ancestors, will she remain a European? Of course not. The dog is still a dog and the African is still an African although raised in foreign, and sometimes, even hostile situations. The essence of us as a people is African. We have much to learn about our great traditions and culture, a culture that has been ignored or taught to us as distasteful or primitive.

African-centered philosophy and treatment has grown out of a movement that views African American behavior not as a deviant from the standards of European American behavior but as a culturally dynamic and viable form in its own right.

There is a proverb that goes: *Because the water is spilled does not mean that the calabash is broken.*

Because we are no longer in Africa or no longer always practice our traditions does not mean that we are not Africans. We are African. And these are some of our strengths.

I would like to start by reviewing some of the key components of African philosophy, or the African belief system, which serve as a foundation for what is called the Afrocentric Theory.

One of the key components in the African belief system is that there is a common spirit or force in all things. It comes out of the concept that God is in us; God is in everything. There is a common spirit or force in all things. There is a proverb that says: *Whatever ends, is in the first place spirit.*

A second key concept is that there is a Supreme force — our God. It is a Supreme force by whatever name you may give this Supreme force — Nyame, Yahweh, Allah, whatever you call God. There is a Supreme force.

A third concept is that there is an essential interconnectedness or interdependence among all things and all people. This reminds me of a story that was told by Rabbi Cohen when he and I sat on a panel in Norfolk, Virginia. It is a story of two people in a boat. Their ship went down and they ended up in a lifeboat together. They had known each other before and had never particularly liked each other. So they sat at opposite ends of the boat facing away from one another. One man heard some noises and turned around to find the other man making holes in the bottom of the boat. He said, "Why are you doing this? Don't you know the boat will sink?" The other man said, "What difference does it make? I am sitting over here and this is my part of the boat and I am making holes here. Where you're sitting is your part of the boat."

Obviously, the boat will sink. The basic concept the rabbi was trying to get across is that there is an interconnectedness or an interdependence among all people and all things.

Another key component in the African belief system is that there is a paramountly and primary importance given to life, as well as a high respect for the multiplicity of form and movement. (Nothing is more important than the human being in the orientation of the African.)

When I was in Africa with my daughters, we found it interesting to see the way the day evolved. The people got up around 8 a.m. and they were off to work or to school or to wherever they were supposed to be for the day. But at noon everybody returned to their homes and stayed until 3 p.m. If you wanted to bank or shop between those hours, forget it; there wasn't anything open. Everybody returned to their homes and they sat down and the women cooked, and they ate together and they napped. At 3 p.m. they went back to work or to school for a couple of hours and then returned home in the evening. What that shows us is the primacy and the importance of family and people.

One other interesting behavior was that there always seemed to be other people coming for dinner or lunch. It didn't matter who you were. If you were there, you ate. There is this high regard and caring for people. It was a wonderful experience to see firsthand.

The first core value of African culture is the high regard for life; the second is cooperation. I have a friend who is very much like this: He does anything that he possibly can to make things easier for another person. It is a concept that is difficult in our average work situation because we are supposed to have a job description and certain functions to carry out. Well, with this particular man, there is no use making a job description. If it needs to be done, he is going to do it regardless of whether it fits his job description. It is a sense of cooperation and a sense that everything must flow together. If it needs to be done, then just do it.

There is a proverb that I used to use with my children about cooperation: *Two birds disputed about a kernel when a third swooped down and carried it off.* (As you can tell, I like proverbs. My children were raised on them. I didn't have to yell and holler at them; I would just give them a proverb. Proverbs are good ways of getting lessons across without giving lectures. Children get sick of lectures. Proverbs have ancient wisdom and they have a sense of moral values.)

Another core value is that of interpersonal connectedness by differences. The proverb that goes with this one is: *The rain does not fall on one roof alone.*

Just like Rabbi Cohen said, you cannot control just one end of the boat. We are all connected and must take care of each other.

Commonality, similarity, and synthesis are other concepts very familiar to the African value system. It means seeing oneself as the same in values as all other people. We all have a common origin and end. I have three teenagers but I always seem to have more than that because ever since my daughter was a young child, she would come home and say this is my play sister or this is my play cousin. So I inherited all kinds of other children. This is very much the sense of the way that young children, black children in particular, relate to each other. We become extended family. My husband told me that when he was young there was a guy about his age who used to come over and play. He was called "Cuz." And it wasn't until he was in his twenties that my husband found out that this man was really not blood-related.

Of course, people at Boys Town certainly know that the extended family concept works. If you don't have good positive relationships with your immediate family, then the extended family is really a very good source of support and help. That is one of the things we found in the Teen Mother program. These girls had been separated from their families because of sexual or physical abuse and neglect. Your family becomes who you are with.

Another core value is restraint, responsibility, and respect. This is the ability to submerge personal desires for the good of the group. Even in disagreements, one is to show respect for the other. This is a concept that is kind of difficult for a lot of materialistic people to get — the merging of one's own personal self for the good of the group.

A sixth and final core value that I would like to share with you is reciprocity. This is the concept of give and take, the law of balance. Another way to say this is *You reap what you sow*, or *What goes around, comes around*.

According to scholar Dr. Lawford Goddard, "An Afrocentric approach to the delivery of educational or social services prevention and treatment, then, reflects the philosophy and practice of the cultural precepts, ideas, and beliefs of Africans and African Americans. The Afrocentric model takes as its fundamental premise the notion that the most effective prevention techniques are those that promote a natural resiliency to pathology."

The promotion of resiliency among youth requires identifying, acknowledging, reinforcing, and celebrating their natural and fundamental attributes. We often try, when working with troubled children and youth, to give them new ideas or formulas, or things that have worked with other people. This is an approach that is often doomed to failure.

Another recommended approach is to assist the youth in identifying, enhancing, and reinforcing that which is natural and normal to them, even though it may often have been held deep inside, usually because of fear. Facing and addressing personal fears often additionally serves to accept the natural gift that God has given them.

My assumption in suggesting this approach is that at some time in a child's life he or she has known love, has had human, caring contact with a nurturing figure. That contact, even if it was brief, is a part of old memories.

The other part of this assumption is that we as humans have "ancestral memory." According to the work of some psychologists, humans and other primates are predisposed to acquire fears that once threatened their ancestors' lives. For example, snakes apparently set off more clinical fears and phobias than either knives or guns. This evolutionary memory, they contend, resulted from those ancestors who rapidly acquired the fear as they were more favored in the natural selection.

One particular study tested monkeys that had been raised in the wild and monkeys that had been raised in a laboratory. The test was done to expose the laboratory-raised monkeys (that had never been exposed to snakes) to a videotape of wild monkeys reacting in horror to snakes. Within 24 minutes, the lab monkeys acquired a fear of snakes. When they tried to evoke fears of other objects like flowers, rabbits, and a crocodile, only the snakes and crocodile elicited the horror.

The latest studies suggest that our bodies, not just our brains, think, reason, and speak. It is a two-way process. The brain does not just command the body and the body follows slavishly. What the brain imparts to the body depends on what the body imparts to the brain.

There are phobias and fears that are inherent. There also are positive things that are inherent. These are part of our ancestral memory. That is why rituals are an important part of reaching young people.

Rituals, traditional and contemporary, can be devised to assist us in transitions in life. Rituals stand apart from ordinary life. Rituals are transformative. Ceremonies, by contrast, are confirmative. Rituals are those things that help us to progress from one stage of life to another. They are symbolic acts that are focused toward fulfilling a specific intention. They signify that something new and possibly unfamiliar is happening.

Frequently, a ritual is like a graduation from school, where young people graduate from one area of school and go to another area of school. They are moving toward an area that is unfamiliar, particularly if they don't have brothers and sisters who have already been through it.

Rituals can increase balance and connectedness within ourselves, with each other, and with the larger rhythms and energies that bring light into our lives. Very simply, rituals create a balance. They allow us to connect with the subconscious. This is why I shared the story of the monkeys and ancestral memory with you. We know that the subconscious mind carries a lot of information of which we aren't consciously aware. When we use rituals, we can begin to pull out unconscious memories and positive behaviors in young people.

I believe that was what happened when we instituted the rituals of Libations and Elder Permission with a lot of the groups with whom we have worked. They began to feel grounded and have a sense of who they were — that this feels right. When someone starts to feel correct about something, their behaviors and attitudes begin to change. Rituals help young people get into that kind of unconscious memory and really pull out what is positive in them. Rituals also help people to get on in their lives after traumas. They help people prepare themselves for a new and often unfamiliar process.

I would like to briefly share with you the concepts of the rites of passage as a developmental process and resiliency approach. I am a psychologist schooled in developmental theory. I learned from the theories of Jung, Freud, and Adler. One of the things that occurred to me after reading about African philosophy was that all of the developmental theory coming from the Western psychologists started with birth and ended with death. There really was no spiritual concept to it. So what I did was superimpose an African-centered view on the developmental life cycle. I came up with what I called the African Spiritual Life Cycle. It is holistic and person-centered and will assist us in viewing spirituality from a cultural, African-centered perspective.

The term "rite of passage" may conjure up some foreign and unknown activities and behaviors. In real life, a passage is something that every person completes, but perhaps without the formality accorded it in other cultures. For example, every person makes the transition from being a child to being an adolescent, which is the entry point to becoming an adult. However, American society does not mark this significant transition with any particular ceremony as many of the world cultures have historically done.

A "rite" is simply a ceremonial or customary series of acts marking some significant occasion. "Passage" means the act or process of the transition or movement from one place or condition to another.

From a holistic perspective, one must view the entire developmental life cycle as a series of transitions or transformations. The African philosophical view of the spiritual/life cycle is in five distinct transition periods: birth, puberty, marriage, eldership, and death. Since social relationships are the key in an African society, these stages are defined by the customary relationships expected of the person in each stage. Every person passes through the series of stages which are marked by ritual and ceremony.

The African Spiritual Life Cycle can be illustrated by picturing a circle of dotted lines. The circle represents the figure whose end is a beginning and whose beginning is an end — a cyclical pattern that repeats and duplicates itself. From an African viewpoint, the circle is not solid, but broken, because there is always an exchange or interplay between the outer and inner world — the physical and spiritual forces. For African people there is no dichotomy between the spiritual and material world, the sacred and the profane. They flow comfortably and interchangeably between both worlds.

Present in the outer or spiritual area is the Creator/God/Yahweh/ Nyame/Allah — whatever name one may call the Supreme Being. Also present in the spiritual world are the ancestors, the dead, the yet-to-be-born, or in general, the whole spiritual community. The inside of the circle represents the cyclical nature of human progression with a spirit entering the physical world through an image of a human baby. Some, too, would argue that conception is the moment that the spirit enters the physical plane.

Birth is the transition from the spiritual world to the physical world. The new person is examined for traces of ancestors or other persons known in past incarnation. Often, the child is given the name of the person he or she physically or spiritually resembles. A celebration marks the entrance of this new being into the midst of the community. The naming ceremony is the time when the community gathers to welcome the new or returned spirit to the physical plane. From this time on, the new spirit/child receives much attention and adoration. Children are included in acknowledgment by adults entering a room, which is unlike the European/Western concept that a child should be seen and not heard. The specialness of each child is cultivated in a multiple parenting framework.

When you look at the concept of birth from an African perspective, the proverb that goes with it is: *Children are the reward of life. Where there are no children, there is no wealth.*

Puberty is the next transition that a person makes in the developmental life cycle. From reading and observation of traditional African culture, we know that the transition from childhood to adolescence is marked by a series of activities to instruct the young person in the responsibilities and privileges of adulthood and with a ceremony marking this passage.

In modern times, some things have not changed. Teens must have a passage to learn "adult" ways, attitudes, and behaviors. Unfortunately, there are many initiators of our young people. In the streets, they include gangs, leaders of the drug culture, or just petty thieves. The proverb that goes with the puberty stage is: *The child that is not raised by its mother is raised by the world.*

114

Marriage is traditionally a very important stage because families form the basis of a healthy, nurturing society. These families will raise children by means of the extended family or by two families joined from the marriage. Therefore, marriage is not just two individuals joining, but also two large extended families coming together. This very often offers more support to the young people and there is less leeway for them to dissolve such a complex set of relationships.

The proverb that goes with this stage is: *The person with family and friends is richer than one with money.*

Eldership is a stage that is basically neglected in the Western cultures that venerate and glorify youth or staying young-looking. The elders of any community have completed all previous activities and rites and have gained significant wisdom to reflectively offer assistance to the community in matters of maintaining harmony and balance. Very often, these older members make up a council of elders who hear and judge cases of conflict from community members and see to the continuation of the traditions of the society. The proverb for this stage is: *When an old person dies, a library burns.*

Death is the final rite of passage, when the physical person returns to the spiritual world. Marked by a ritual of passing, the funeral is attended by the community out of respect for the family of the departed. The person's life is reviewed and expressions of grief and release are expected. It is the strong belief that his or her being will remain in the community of ancestors until all persons who knew him or her while living also have passed. Ancestors are called upon by the living for help and guidance. The ancestor then moves to the community of spirits.

The proverb that goes with this stage says: *Birth is not a beginning and death is not an end.*

Virtue was an essential part of the growth process. Some of the most ancient traditions included the development of the qualities that put the neophyte in harmony with people, nature, and God. The original educational system, then, goes back to Khemet (Egypt) where the mission of education was a spiritual goal — that is, to become God-like or one with the Creator. We teach these ancient traditional values, which always include spiritualism, when providing rite of passage experiences for young people.

In traditional societies in Africa, Australia, and among peoples who conducted rites of passage for their youth, there were five steps and three major functions of the rites of passage.

Step 1 is to prepare the sacred ground (finding a place away from the community, erecting enclosures, marking paths or ceremonial circles, providing spiritual cleansing of the area, etc.). The symbol of the sacred ground was the image of the world and the consecrated presence of God. The sacred area symbolized the place and the time when God or the ancestors founded the initiation ceremonies. It was reliving the Time and the Place when God provided the initiation.

Step 2 is the separation from the mother. Most of the anthropological and sociological literature focuses on the male and how the maternal relationship is abruptly severed when it is time for him to become a man.

Step 3 is initiatory death. It was believed that boys needed to learn the lesson for becoming men. Therefore, it was also important that the men take the boys to the prepared sacred ground. The men would sometimes surprise the boys and take them at night when no one was awake. There was some fear involved. The concept is linked with the idea of initiatory death because it is the death of the child and the rebirth of the person as an adult. Some of the concepts then — death, darkness, the unknown — are brought out if you look at the concept of moving from the darkness to the light, from the profane to the sacred. The passage requires the death of one life to gain access to another.

Step 4 contains initiatory ordeals. These ordeals, again, are linked to the concept of moving from darkness to light, from the unknown to the known. It is Divinity that restores life and confers sexuality and fertility. These rituals may include not being permitted to speak, not feeding oneself, sight to the ground, fasting, and so on, to prove physical and spiritual strength.

Step 5 is the initiatory rebirth or collective regeneration. It is the symbol of awakening and ascension. The boy or girl returns to life and is a new person to the community.

There also are three important functions that these traditional rites serve:

The first function is that the initiates must establish their relationship with God. When the time comes for the rite of passage, it is imperative that the young people understand what spiritual development means to their future lives — to know God is the number one function of the rite of passage.

The second function is to impart the Sacred History. The Sacred History means that young people must learn the history that is specific to their people. To African Americans, this goes from Khemet, to West Africa, to the times when we were kings and queens, to a period of enslavement, to a period when we were oppressed, and now moving again to re-ascension and understanding of who we are as cultural people.

The third important function is to teach young people their roles — for males, that of husband and father; for females, that of wife and mother.

The adolescent rite of passage, as it is called in African American communities, is the supervised developmental and educational process that assists young people toward the knowledge and acceptance of responsibilities, privileges, and duties of a person in the African American community. It is a way to bring our children back into the ways of the traditionally supportive African American community. Many parents and families seek to give their children the basic nurturing, guidance, resources, and information needed for passage to adulthood. It should be noted, however, that the routine of adolescent development — turning youth into adults — proceeds regardless of responsible adult input.

Slavery and oppression have had devastating effects on the development and growth of Americans of African descent, including the youth. This is one of the problems that we as African Americans continue to have. The slave mentality exists today among people who have been oppressed. I would like to share with you Kenneth Stampp's concept of "How to Make a Slave."

The master had to establish and maintain strict discipline. The slave had to obey at all times, under all circumstances, without question. The whites wanted unconditional surrender and the slave must understand that whites govern absolutely.

Implant in the slaves a consciousness of personal inferiority. The slaves were to know and keep their places. They should feel a difference between the whites and the slaves. The slaves should understand that bondage was a natural status for colored people.

The slaves should understand that their African ancestry tainted them and their color was a badge of degradation.

The slaves should have fear, awe, and obedience for the master. Fear and obedience are woven into the very nature of the slave.

The slave should take an interest in the master's businesses. The slaves should accept the master's standards of good conduct and feel that advancement of white interest is the same as advancement of theirs.

The slave should feel helplessness. The slave needed to depend on the whites for everything and could do nothing without them.

These attitudes and behaviors remain in oppressed and formerly enslaved peoples.

The child who is not raised by its mother will be raised by the world.

One of the reasons for the increase in gangs and gang activity is that these social units take the place of families and communities that are dysfunctional or negligent in raising young people.

"Gangs" have been defined as "collectivities that have an inclination toward disruptive, antisocial, or criminal behavior." The gang also offers what every person wants and needs — friendship, a sense of belonging, discipline and boundaries, nurturing and bonding, security, support, a means to financial income, and the ritual of passage. Of course, the disadvantages of gang culture are the violence, crime, and the link to the drug culture.

Rites of passage among African Americans are quickly becoming popular. The use of adolescent rite of passage is sweeping African American communities in an effort to reduce the involvement of young people in substance abuse, crime, violence, gangs, and other detrimental life experiences.

Rites of passage can be applied in churches, schools, community centers, housing communities, residential homes, and therapeutic centers. Young people could possibly undergo two or more rites at the time of puberty — one in their school, one in their church, and one in the community or housing center.

Regardless of race, gender, ethnicity, socioeconomic situation, or geographic location, there are some principles that we must instill in all our children and youth.

1. The principle of understanding self. We must guide our young people toward an understanding of their family and cultural origins. Culture becomes a grounding and the family is the stabilizer. Every person must seek wholeness, not only in the development of the four parts of self, but also with the interrelated, interconnected universe. *A tree cannot stand without its roots.*

2. The principle of elder respect. We must make our communities intergenerational so that respect for our elders becomes a way of life. We need to include elders in our lives so that young people have a balanced view of the life cycle and understand the importance of respect for those who have made paths for us. *A single conversation with a wise man is better than ten years' mere study of books.*

3. The principles of discipline and virtue. We must instill values in all our youth. Values are the way humans pattern and use their energy. If there is imbalance between ourselves and others, we cannot continue to grow into our true human potential. Thus, this

imbalance can cause the death of individuals and communities. *Kindness is a loan, not a gift.*

4. The principle of trust. We must be consistent caretakers for our children. There is no other way for them to learn the trust and bonding necessary to become productive citizens. *The woman who uses her sister as her hairdresser needs no mirror.*

5. The principle of cooperation. Our society is very competitive. But like the human body, things always function and perform better when all parts, no matter how great or small, work in harmony with the others. *One finger cannot wash your face.*

6. The principle of balance. Observe moderation and balance in all things. Honor the balance of nature, including the need for gender balance in the lives of our children. *If blackberries make you sick, you will not eat them again.*

In closing, I would like to applaud you for your commitment, your time, your interest, and your investment in our most precious resource — our nation's youth.

I leave you with a proverb to live by: *Do not consider any vice as trivial, and therefore practice it; do not consider any virtue as unimportant, and therefore neglect it.*

DR. NSENGA WARFIELD-COPPOCK is an organizational psychologist who is president of Baobob Associates, Inc. in Washington, D.C. She is the author, co-author, or editor of four books addressing rites of passage within the African American community. These books include **Afrocentric Theory and Applications; Volumes 1 and 2: Adolescent Rites of Passage,** *and* **Images of African Sisterhood: Initiation and Rites of Passage to Womanhood** *(all published by Baobab Associates). Her essay in this volume was first presented at the 1993 symposium, "Fostering Spiritual Growth Among At-Risk Youth: Multicultural Perspectives."*

REFERENCES

Stampp, K.M. (1956). In **The peculiar institution: Slavery in the ante-bellum South** (1st edition). New York: Knopf.

CHAPTER SEVEN

Portrait of Asian American Youth: Cultural Issues for Ministry

REV. DONALD NG

A computer expert, a scientist, a math student, a martial arts master, a Chinese restaurant worker, a foreigner, a foreign student, an immigrant, a Japanese business-man or tourist. A person who is quiet, shy, won't speak up in groups, plays tennis or Ping Pong, speaks with an accent, knows where the best Chinese restaurants are, knows the whereabouts of any Asian person living in his or her home city, has ancestors from some faraway land in the Orient.

These are just a few of the most common perceptions people might have when they see or meet an Asian American person. When we think of Asians, a multiplicity of images come to mind. We may think of nationalities, language groups, regional home-lands, generational categories, facial features, physique and pigmen-tation characteristics, and many other images.

The term "Asian American" represents a very diverse group of people. There are Burmese, Cambodian, Chinese, Filipino, Hmong, Indian, Indonesian, Japanese, Korean, Laotian, Malaysian, Mien, Pacific Islanders, Singaporean, Thai, Vietnamese, and others. Although the experiences of some of the groups may be similar, each has a distinct culture, language, and history.

A few years ago, there was a movie called *The Brother From Another Planet.* The movie begins with a black man swimming out of New York City harbor with the Statue of Liberty and the World

Trade Center in the background. He crawls onto Ellis Island and has the ability to sense and feel all the cries, pain, struggles, questions, and fears of the European immigrants who were detained on the island before they were allowed to come on the mainland. Not surprisingly, the black man finds refuge in Harlem and faces the same kind of racial prejudice and discrimination experienced by African Americans. In many ways, Asian Americans are like the brother from another planet. They find themselves in a new world, oftentimes without friends and acceptance.

Today, Asian Americans belong to the fastest-growing ethnic minority group in the United States. According to John Naisbitt's *Trend Letter* (May 10, 1990), "Asian Americans skyrocketed from 3.7 million residents in 1980 to more than 6.5 million today, a 71 percent increase — seven times the general population expansion. By the year 2000, four of every 100 U.S. residents will be Asian Americans. Bolstered by a continuing immigration wave through this decade, the number of Japanese, Chinese, Filipinos, Koreans, Vietnamese, Cambodians, and other Asian residents will exceed 10 million in the new millennium."

Here are some startling facts from Naisbitt:

- California, the nation's gateway to the booming Pacific Rim and home to nearly 3 million Asian Americans, has the largest concentration.
- Half of Monterey Park's residents are of Chinese descent.
- The world's largest Korean community outside Korea can be found in Los Angeles. Some 300,000 Koreans live in the city's Koreantown.
- If you look in San Jose's phone book, you'll find far more people named Nguyen, a Vietnamese surname, than Jones.

In addition to the dramatic population growth of Asian Americans that has caught the attention of the media, Asian Americans are said to be more affluent, on the average, than any other racial or ethnic group, including whites. Furthermore, Asians have been credited with having the highest level of education of all other groups: Among adults 25 or older, 14 percent of Asians have five or more years of college, compared with only 9 percent of all Americans. Although these statistics are marveled at by entrepreneurs for new markets and misused to create a "model minority" myth, there are many exceptions and particularities to those figures that raise questions about the validity of these assertions.

For example, one exception to the above statistics is the validity of understanding Asian Americans as a monolithic group. Usually, the non-Asian, for whatever reason, would prefer to treat all Asians alike. Subsequently, there has been increasing media coverage on the identity of Asian Americans as a group. Susmu Awanohara of Los Angeles, writing in the *Far Eastern Review*, said:

"The sheer heterogeneity of Asian Americans makes it hard for them to consolidate political power. They are divided into at least half a dozen major ethnic groups, each of which is further subdivided according to the time of arrival, social origins, religious and factional affiliations."

The nomenclature of "Asian Americans" was first introduced in the 1960s for advocating legislation favoring the interests of Asians. By grouping together, Asians had political clout to petition for census-driven policy-making leading to the establishment of affirmative action goals and federal aid to Asian American communities. Although the name is being used more today, most people do not call themselves Asian Americans except for the reasons stated earlier. In most cases, they tend to describe themselves in specific, rather than general, terms.

I am a second-generation Chinese American. In the Chinese culture, we have an acronym — ABC. It doesn't refer only to the American Baptist Churches; it also refers to American-Born Chinese. It would be even more derogatory for a Chinese elder to call me Jook Sing instead of Ju Gak. Jook is the Chinese word for bamboo, and Jook Sing is the hollow part of the bamboo. As you cut the bamboo in half, there are hollow sections. But every now and then, usually a foot apart, there are knots, and Ju Gak means "the knot." Jook Sing means "the hollow part." Now they call me Jook Sing because I was born in the United States. Even though I look Asian on the outside, I'm hollow on the inside — I don't appreciate my Chinese traditions and rituals. Those who are born in Asia are referred to as Jook Gak because they are both Asian on the outside as well as Asian on the inside.

Our self-descriptions are further complicated by likes and dislikes, experiences, interests, abilities, skills, vocation, etc. For example, as a Chinese American, I can neither read nor write Chinese, but I can still speak Toisanese with my mother. Sometimes, I feel I can't read, write, or even speak English any better! As a Chinese American, I can wolf down a hot dog and Coke in Fenway Park as well as pick the meat off oxtails stewed in black beans and drink a cup of chrysanthemum tea in my mother's house.

Acquiring a more complete understanding of the histories and concerns of each of the different Asian American groups will definitely enable you to engage in more effective ministries for youth. I have merely scratched the surface with my introductory comments. However, I would recommend Ronald Takaki's, *Strangers From a Different Shore, A History of Asian Americans*, published in 1989. Takaki looks at Asian Americans as a cultural group, breaks them down as Asian groups, and discusses the issues that each group faces. The book is a good resource for anyone who ministers to Asian American youth.

The histories of Asian Americans are rooted in America's developing national identity and expanding economic needs. To understand why Asian Americans came to the United States, you must first understand that there is both a national identity issue as well as an economic issue. On the one hand, Asian laborers have been deliberately sought to meet the growing needs of American businesses. On the other hand, Asians have been perceived as inhuman or subhuman, a threat to racial purity, un-American, and unassimilable.

America's changing perception of Asians, or for that matter of any racial/ethnic group, is based on America's self-identity and the process known as "Americanization." Throughout U.S. history, there have been different policies in the Americanizing of new immigrants and racial/ethnic people. According to Philip Gleason, in an article in the *Harvard Encyclopedia of Racial Ethnic Groups*, it was an ideological quality that was important during the colonial period in determining the definition of an American identity. According to Gleason:

"To be or become American, a person did not have to be of any particular national, linguistic, religious, or ethnic background. All he had to do was to commit himself to the political ideology centered on the abstract ideals of liberty, equality and republicanism."

In the first half of the 1800s, a large influx of European immigrants who were Roman Catholics created bitter bursts of nativism. Organized political efforts to secure public funds to support Catholic education was perhaps the most highly charged issue of all. In order to protect their religion from nativistic attacks, it was imperative for Catholics to distinguish between nationality and the Catholic faith, so that immigrants would not abandon their faith in the process of Americanization. To be Catholic is not to be un-American.

In the latter half of the 1800s, we begin to see the elements of race and ethnicity becoming central to the discussion of nationality. This was the period when large numbers of Chinese immigrants arrived in the United States.

I've already mentioned that I am an American-born Chinese. I also should mention that my parents are from China and that my father served in the U.S. Army during World War II after coming to the United States. He left my mother and older brother in China and came to the United States to work and have enough economic success so that he could eventually return to China to live out the rest of his life. The other point I want to make is that both my paternal and maternal grandfathers worked in the United States as laborers and they too left their families in China. This was a very common way for Chinese to immigrate to the United States. It is interesting that a lot of people say to us, "Why don't you go home to where you came from?" Well, my grandparents, as well as my father, really had no intentions to stay here, but the turn of history almost made it impossible for them to return. My father actually was drafted by the United States Army during World War II and served as a corporal in Germany. Eventually, because he served honorably in the United States Army, he became a citizen and then was able to sponsor my mother and older brother so they could come to the United States. That is some personal history about how some Chinese came to the States.

The discussion of "ethnicity in the American identity" can be interpreted in four concepts:

1. The melting pot
2. Americanization
3. Anglo-Saxon racialism
4. Cultural pluralism

I'll discuss these four concepts very briefly as a frame of reference to the understanding of Asian Americans in general and Asian American youth specifically.

For many years, the term "melting pot" was the most popular symbol for ethnic integration in society. In 1909, Israel Zangwill opened his play, *The Melting Pot*, in New York. As the words suggest, Old World nationalities should be forgotten in the United States and these cultural elements should be fused together in the creation of a new and superior American nationality. During this time, it was believed by the scientific community that mixed peoples were superior to those from a single strain. The melting pot was simply a theory of assimilation. The idea was that immigrants would change and adopt the traditions of the dominant culture. Whatever survived the blending would become a part of the melting pot.

After the symbol of the melting pot was discredited, the term "Americanization" became attached to the movement to foster an American identity. There were many expressions of Americanization. Schools taught citizenship responsibilities, hygiene, domestic science, and industrial arts. During World War I, the National Americanization Committee (NAC) moved in the direction of forced assimilation. With the Red Scare, patriotic groups intensified their Americanization programs to inculcate the great masses of immigrants.

Anglo-Saxon racialism began as a form of ethnic pride. Eventually, it became a much harsher form of racism. The science of eugenics introduced scientific racism, which was a matter of biological and anthropological determinism.

In 1915, Horace M. Kallen first presented the term "cultural pluralism" to designate an anti-assimilationist viewpoint. Kallen called for a "federation of nationalities." He held the point that ethnic nationalities neither should nor could be transformed into any generic American nationality. Cultural pluralism began to lose its conceptual rigor when it was difficult to operationalize unity within diversity.

The purpose of this article is to place the journeys of Asian Americans in the broader context of American life and history. During most of the 19th century, when national identity was not threatened by ethnic diversity, more tolerant and inclusive versions of the melting pot in society were permitted. However, an uneasiness for immigrants grew in the 1890s as the flood of new immigration was coupled in the public mind with various forms of social, economic, and political unrest. The crisis of World War I in the early 20th century led to more active forms of Americanization and racism. After restrictions had been accomplished, Americans once again became more relaxed about national identity.

The issue in understanding Asian American youth for ministry is often based on the question, "What is the political, economic, sociological, and cultural milieu in America that may affect Asian Americans?" The U.S. national debt, sluggish economy, unemployment, competition from Japanese businesses, the apparent Asian American influence, and the "buying out" of American symbols of power all are factors which have created anti-Asian violence. The murder of Vincent Chin in Detroit several years ago is a graphic example.

Chin was a young Chinese American man who was in a bar during a bachelor party two weeks before his wedding. He was mistaken by two auto workers as a Japanese, and there was some arguing in the bar about the American economy and how the United States car industry has been destroyed because of Japanese imports. Eventually, a man and his son-in-law who both had been laid off from the auto industry chased Chin down in their car and killed him with a baseball bat they had in the trunk. These two men were convicted, but they were placed on probation for three years and were fined only $3,750 for the death of Vincent Chin. This is the political, economic, and sociological environment that Asian American youth find themselves in.

Let me say here that every country is guilty of nativism and ethnocentrism. For example, the Chinese characters for China mean "middle kingdom." This implies that everything swirls around China. My use of Chin's death is not meant to be critical or judgmental because even my parents have racist attitudes from being brought up in a culture that taught that to be Chinese is to be superior.

Similarly, Americans have grown up learning the Mercator depiction of the earth, which places the Western Hemisphere in the center and arranges the other continents according to maritime lines. Most classroom maps show the United States and the Northern Hemisphere right in the middle, South America at the bottom, and Asia split, so that half is on the left side and half is on the right side. I can never find China because it is on both sides. As we grow up in school, this image of the world leads us to think of America as being the center of the universe. It builds on what the American national identity is all about.

The newer Peter's Projection map attempts to offer another view of the world from the perspective of land masses. This type of map shows the continents of Africa and South America as much larger than the Northern Hemisphere. (I urge educators to buy this type of map because it helps youth to think in more global terms.)

Given this, it is not surprising that white Americans, and I would say more recently, African Americans, perceive Asian Americans as not fitting the definition of what an American is. I include African Americans because of the recent riots in Los Angeles and the racial misunderstanding there, especially between African Americans and Korean Americans. We saw this in Los Angeles, and we see this all over the country. When you see a white person or an African American person, you assume that the person is an American; when you see an Asian American, your first inclination is that the person is a foreigner.

My wife once courteously gave an older woman her parking spot in front of the post office. When they saw each other inside, the woman said, "Thank you. Where are you from?" A white person or a black person wouldn't be asked that question. But Asians are constantly asked that question. When I tell someone I'm from Boston, that's not adequate. Because then the person will always ask the question, "Well, where are you really from?" And being the nice person that I am, I always give in and say that my parents are from China but I was born in Boston. And I try to make it a teachable moment to educate as many people as possible.

Depending on the prevalent political, economical, sociological, and perhaps, religious milieu that may exist in society at any given time, people's attitudes toward or their perceptions of Asian Americans may differ. To illustrate, society may perceive Asians as either FRIEND or FOE. On the other hand, Asian Americans may perceive themselves as either CITIZEN or ALIEN. The following chart illustrates the matrix of possible ways Asian Americans are perceived in America.

Society's Perception of Asian Americans

		FRIEND	FOE
	CITIZEN	Co-worker	Competitor
Self-Perceptions		(Kindness)	(Envy)
of Asian Americans			
	ALIEN	Consumer	Scab
		(Indifference)	(Rage)

131

I've tried to lay out historically how at times Asians are valued when they are meeting some economic labor needs, and then when Asian Americans become too much of a threat either because they have grown in numbers or they have achieved in certain kinds of job security, they are quite often seen as a threat.

This is an economic model simply because I feel that much of the persecution Asian Americans have experienced has been primarily based on economic factors. If society perceives Asians as friends and if Asians perceive themselves as citizens who are going to contribute to the life of the country, then they see each other mutually as co-workers. There is a sense of kindness there. For example, in my employment with the American Baptist Churches, I have worked in the same office for 15 years. My name is familiar, I don't pose a threat, and other employees see me as a friend. And because I have been indebted to my denomination for who I am, I see myself as a citizen of the United States as well as a real member of this denomination. So kindness is exchanged. But when this society perceives an Asian as a foe, then we become competitors and society expresses envy. The worst that could happen is that Asian Americans could perceive themselves as aliens and society could perceive Asians as foes. Then society perceives Asians as scabs, which is the name given to people who are hired to break a labor strike, and there is actually rage. Violence is directed at Asian laborers as well as at whoever has displaced workers in that labor operation. When Asians perceive themselves only as aliens — perhaps you can say they are consumers — a sense of indifference occurs. This economic model illustrating how Asian Americans are perceived differently, depending on the broader circumstances, helps us to recognize the complexity in the understanding of effective ministry with Asian American youth. Let us now focus more specifically on Asian American youth.

Chinese philosophy is based on the theme of "balance" or what is known as the "yin and the yang." When I was a child and would get sick after eating too much fried food, my mother would always cook up this translucent paste called "thick flour" to counterbalance the fried food. For some unknown reason, the stuff works. (My mother still lives in Boston; she is about 88 years old. I still have some of the translucent paste at home, so when I get sick from eating too much fried chicken, I will work up this stuff and try to bring more balance to my biological system.)

When we talk about the strengths and concerns of cultural groups, we also can see that for every strength that can be identified, there also is a concern, or possibly a weakness. Since eating healthier is in, I'll refer to cultural negatives as "fried foods" and cultural positives as "thick flour." These cultural strengths and their accompanying weaknesses are: cultural pride and Asian racialism; industriousness and impersonal relationships; family cohesion and loss of individuality; belonging and shame; and social adaptability and self-hate.

Cultural pride and Asian racialism. Earlier I mentioned that the word "China" means "middle kingdom." Built into the mindset of the Chinese is the belief of superiority. The Great Wall was constructed to prevent barbarians from coming in. Asian racialism can be seen in the ethnic communities of American cities that were once very isolated from the rest of the city. In some major cities, there are Chinatowns or Japantowns. I know that when I grew up in Boston, Chinatown was a separate city. The Boston Police Department never entered Chinatown unless there was a killing; then police came in to remove the corpse. There was this isolation between the Asian community and the rest of the city.

The more recent arrival of Korean Americans has sparked racial violence among neighbors that to some extent stems from the desire of the Korean Americans to be apart from their neighbors. As long as Asian Americans, and for that matter, any group, hold to the view that they are better than others, such racially motivated violence will persist. Asian Americans are not exempt from racism.

In what we have called "Asian racialism," we also can affirm cultural pride. The variety and richness of cultural rituals and traditions provide any human community a firsthand witness to God's wonderful creation.

133

The fabric of American culture has been interwoven with Asian traditions: Chinese New Year, foods, and language. And more importantly, cultural pride serves as the source of strength and values for Asian American children and youth as they work on identity formation as persons of color. Parents are able to explain to their children why their hair cannot be naturally curly like their friends' hair. (My son came home one time and said he'd like to have a little curl on his head; he wanted to be like Superman. We had to tell him and share with him that that is not the way he is. That is cultural pride through the education of where he has come from.) Family elders can spin tales that instruct the young in their responsibilities as members of the clan.

Industriousness and impersonal relationships. Confucianism teaches that prosperity and good fortunes are results of hard work. The stereotype of the hard-working Asian is rooted in this philosophy. Although tremendous gains by Asian Americans have usually meant that all family members work long hours in often menial jobs, the negative effect is the erosion of family interpersonal relationships.

The most recent census indicates that Asian American income levels are the highest. But it does not show that children and young people usually contribute to that income. And when the census takers take the census or they go into income taxes, they do not distinguish the fact that those income amounts have been generated by not just two people, but usually by three or four members of the family who work to contribute to that income. Many parents work 18-hour shifts, leaving children to fend for themselves. The goal is to make money for a more comfortable lifestyle and to be able to afford to send all the children to the best colleges in the nation. By expressing the latter reason, most children would submissively retract their pleas for parents to play with them.

The strength of Asian American industriousness has stood up against great odds of discrimination and persecution. At the expense of family togetherness, Asian Americans have made a name for themselves in being industrious. One is reminded of the heroic risks Chinese railroad workers took at Donner's Pass to build the transcontinental railroad.

Family cohesion and loss of individuality. Asian American youth are frequently reared to examine the impact of their individual actions on their families' reputations. The expectations parents and other family members have for youth often take priority over individual choices and ideas. Family gatherings are more important than school functions. The overwhelming importance placed on what is good for the family occasionally denies Asian American youth confidence in individual decision-making. Many Asian American parents play an influential role in choosing what college their children will attend. This active involvement in a child's college education has occasionally created so much pressure to succeed that Asian American youth have one of the highest suicide rates in the country. Parents literally live out their lives again in their children's lives, particularly if the parents did not have the opportunity to attend college.

With the loss of helping young people make individual decisions, there is family cohesion. Now that may sound contradictory because I just stated that the interpersonalness of family has been broken down because family members work a lot. But I am talking about the fact that there is a difference between family cohesion and family relationships. Asian families tend to stay together. But I would say that the quality of family life is quite different. Family members stick together because of obligation for one another. Parents, especially fathers, take a very highly structural patriarchal role in making sure families do not stray from the values that they have laid out. But that does not necessarily mean there is a real sense of interpersonalness between parents, or between parents and their children, or even among children. Well-defined roles and responsibilities help children and youth share in the affairs of life. This is family cohesion. When I was growing up, I knew what my limits were. I guess it's important to live in some kind of structural unit, to know what is acceptable and what is not. Youth learn at an early age the values of community and service to others. Selfishness is frowned upon. And as Mr. Spock of *Star Trek* would say: "The good of the many outweighs the good of the one."

Belonging and shame. Growing up as a Chinese American, I was constantly reminded by my father to not bring shame upon my family. He would tell me whatever I did at school or in town, I represented him. (I say this to my son now. It's wonderful.) And if I did something to embarrass my father, I would in fact be saying that he had not fulfilled his duties as a father. Asian American youth frequently defer or pass up opportunities for new challenges out of fear of failure, which would bring shame to the entire household.

It is difficult to get Asian youth to volunteer for new things. Very rarely will you see young people volunteering to do extracurricular things because they fear it will cause them to fail academically. They believe the time they need to spend on school work is more important because their parents believe that doing well in school takes priority over anything else.

One of my greatest and most traumatic experiences occurred when I was in the third grade. I was very shy, a stereotype of a shy, quiet, Chinese boy. My third-grade teacher knew that I knew the answer to her question, but I was so afraid to speak in class that I never offered to give the answer. So my teacher said, "Donald, stand up." So I stood up and she took me by the arm and shook me and stated, "I want the answer out of you. Give me an answer." And obviously, my yellow skin turned to red. I was so embarrassed and I cried in front of my classmates. It was difficult for me to volunteer an answer even though I knew it. This points out the cultural upbringing of Asian American youth. Even one who was born in the United States.

Designing educational methods that will recognize the variety of educational needs of African American, Asian American, Native American, and Hispanic American students, as well as European American students, would lift up the importance of learning for your students. Don't pretend that one method is going to be universally effective for everyone. That is very important.

Shame may be an effective motivator for discipline. But shame also can stifle creativity and the will to even try. In exchange for not shaming the family, Asian American culture nurtures a deep sense of belonging. In Asian neighborhoods, there are family associations that offer connectiveness with everyone who has the same last name. Family obligations foster family reunion, gift-giving, and support for one another, especially in economic crises. The feeling of belonging is not only an essential value in Asian American culture, but also is essential for youth development.

Social adaptability and self-hate. Recently, much has been said about the media's ability to engineer public opinion. For a long time, the media of television and cinema have engineered for the American public the positive and negative images of what a woman should be, what a man should be, and what an Asian American should be. There are no Asian Americans playing lead roles on TV. And what often is portrayed are negative stereotypical images of Asians as martial arts fighters, drug warlords, and prostitutes. Asian American youth grow up with few, if any, strong, positive role models of Asian Americans in the mainstream of American life. Gradually, Asian American youth begin to feel that to be Asian is to be ugly. Asian American girls have plastic surgery to have larger eyes and thinner noses. Asian American boys who aspire to be taller and more muscular are usually disappointed because genetically they have small physiques. I always wanted to be taller when I was growing up, and I guess I stopped growing some time ago.

These are only a few examples of the low self-esteem and self-hate found in many Asian American youth. They want to be "more white" if they can. The controversy over whether figure skater Kristi Yamaguchi can pick up corporate sponsors as a Japanese American points to this issue of what the American identity is today.

Asian Americans' intense desire to be Americanized also has prepared them to be effective in social adaptability. Asian Americans have demonstrated the ability to function well in multiple kinds of settings by applying the appropriate norms and mannerisms in different settings. For example, an Asian American youth may attend a multi-ethnic central high school, work after school at McDonald's, cook dinner for the family (which includes grandmother who can speak only an Asian language), attend language school on Saturday morning, and date a white friend. The amphibious nature of Asian Americans who live in a hyphenated world of both what is American and Asian is a cultural strength.

These five polarities of cultural strengths and weaknesses, or "thick flour" and "fried foods," are in no way a complete description of Asian American gifts and concerns. However, they probably do represent the primary issues facing our ministry to and with Asian American youth. Given these concerns, are Asian American youth at risk? According to the Search Institute and Boys Town, the physical, psychological, and spiritual development of adolescents is said to be at risk if they engage in three or more of the following behaviors: alcohol use, binge drinking, marijuana use, recent contemplation of suicide, and sexual intercourse. Additional at-risk behaviors include experiences of depression, cocaine or other abusive drug use, aggression (hitting or beating up others six or more times during the past year), theft, and trouble in school.

There is no doubt in my mind that Asian American youth who are involved in these behaviors are being placed at risk for their lives. Some of them are in your own parishes, communities, and schools. I would venture to say, however, that an effective response to Asian American youth necessitates a strategy that is different from the dominant cultural understanding of at-risk youth. There are two factors that support my thinking: culture and discrimination.

For the most part, cultural values play a significant role in the lives of Asian American youth. Although cultural pride, family cohesion, and belonging can support an Asian American youth's journey through life, they also can be unbearingly oppressive and relentless. Youth are prevented from showing their unique identities. (I mentioned earlier that I always remind my son that when he goes out he represents me and he can't bring shame to the family. But as an educator and one who majored in psychology in college, I try to encourage my son and my daughter to show their uniqueness, to empower them and enable them to be who they are for themselves and not just an extension of who I am.)

With these types of restrictions, some Asian American youth

live under so much pressure to be successful in school that committing suicide is the only way out. This is by far one of the most identifiable at-risk behaviors of Asian youth. Many of the young people who do commit suicide are in college or in graduate education. The unfortunate thing is that Asian Americans have a distaste for therapy or counseling. They don't want to go to a therapist because in Asian culture, going to a therapist is as bad as saying that you are already tainted for life. It is a bad label that you don't want. So young people, especially those who are trying to succeed academically, do not find a way out except to take their own lives.

Others do things that are not true to their own gifts and to their own interests and abilities. Some Asian Americans agree to pursue college majors and professions that might give the family name greater honor and status, rather than majors or professions the students enjoy. When I was growing up, my father said, "Be an engineer because you don't need to speak English. You can just work with things. Math is a universal language, and you will be successful." My high school counselor wanted me to go to Northeastern so I could be an engineer.

I have always wondered why there are so many artists, poets, philosophers, and political leaders in China, and why Asian Americans are mostly computer programmers, accountants, lab researchers, and math teachers.

For Asian American youth, the pressures from cultural realities can place them at risk. My challenge to educators is to not encourage Asian American youth to go into fields that have been culturally stereotypical. Instead, encourage them to be architects, teachers, politicians, ministers, and priests.

The second at-risk factor, which is not unique to Asian American youth but which also affects other racial ethnic people, is prejudice and discrimination. As long as the dominant culture and its groups are unwilling to invite the contributions of Asian Americans to be a legitimate part of the national identity, Asian American youth will continue to experience self-hatred and anti-Asian violence. They will continue to feel marginalized and on the fringe of life. We are reminded of events in history that reinforced the belief that Asian lives don't count: dropping the atomic bomb on Hiroshima; the internment of more than 100,000 Americans of Japanese descent during World War II; and more recently, the baseball bat killing of Vincent Chin in Detroit by auto workers who blamed him for Japanese imports and the demise of the Big Three automakers. This concerns me greatly because even today, Asian Americans do not fit into the American national identity. We see that in addition to the earlier-mentioned at-risk behaviors that have been identified by Boys Town and the Search Institute, Asian American youth also can be affected by cultural pressures and racial discrimination.

What can we do? There are 10 responses that I would like to propose for people who work with or teach Asian American youth.

1. Become acquainted with the Asian Americans in your community. Know who they are. You will find Korean American leaders, Chinese American leaders, and Hmong community leaders. There are many Cambodian tribal leaders who became leaders in the United States. I know that in Kansas City and in Minnesota there are many Southeast Asians. They probably will not want to interact with you because of their own sense of being separate and being insulated from the Western culture. They are afraid of losing their tradition. But you must involve them in accepting civic responsibilities for their own immediate community, as well as being a part of the larger metropolitan area. Without such a commitment, they will continue to be disenfranchised and isolated from the mainstream of American life.

2. Avoid stereotypes of Asian Americans. What you think an Asian American is, is probably incorrect. Asian Americans are a very diverse group of people; you must find out who they are.

3. Provide support and sensitivity to the dilemmas Asian American youth face in balancing the expectations of individual and

family values, and of American and Asian values. Asian American young people will find themselves in dilemmas. That tension is part of who they are; your sensitivity and support in those situations is important.

4. Affirm positive self-identity in Asian American youth. Give praise and affirmations for accomplishments and uniqueness. Make a commitment to eradicate a limited image of beauty portrayed in the media and petition for the inclusion of a multicultural representation of all youth. When you design education materials, include representations of young people of various backgrounds, races, and cultures.

5. Encourage Asian American youth to discover their gifts in order to explore new possibilities for careers and vocations.

6. Serve as mentors and role models for Asian American youth. All young people are seeking journey partners with whom they can share their hopes, concerns, and dreams. Life can be an easier journey with someone who may know where to turn and who knows where the potholes are.

7. Incorporate the themes of Asian American history and culture in your curriculum and programs. Make the learning of the American experience full of voices and perspectives that have been silenced in the past. This also applies to African American history, Hispanic American history, and a variety of Native American history. Create a global world view and show how your students fit in.

8. Address prejudice, discrimination, and racially motivated violence directly, with no exceptions. There is no place for racism in education or in the church. As an educator, you must address this issue, because if you don't, you have already indirectly sent the message to that minority or racial ethnic child or young person that he or she does not count. You have already lost the trust and credibility

to be part of that young person's life. When we are capable of dealing with racial discrimination, we begin to model our conviction for the human rights of all people.

9. Advocate for a multicultural understanding of America's national identity rather than accepting the images from the past. If we believe that God has truly created such a masterpiece of diversity of cultures and traditions, let us begin to celebrate that creation by welcoming all to participate in sharing God's blessings.

10. Foster Asian American theologizing with youth. Spiritual formation in Asian American youth should include the task of living theology in both word and deed. We can help young people understand the Scriptures from an Asian American perspective. And in doing that, we facilitate opportunities for youth to be involved in mission and ministry.

> *The REV. DONALD NG is director of Education for Discipleship for the American Baptist Churches in Valley Forge, Pennsylvania. He is editor of the book,* **Asian Pacific American Youth Ministry.** *He also has specialized in multicultural youth ministry and has led numerous training events on ministry with Asian-Pacific Americans. His essay in this volume was presented at the 1993 symposium, "Fostering Spiritual Growth Among At-Risk Youth: Multicultural Perspectives."*

REFERENCES

Takaki, R. (1989). **Strangers from a different shore: A history of Asian Americans.** Boston: Little Brown.

Gleason, P. (1980). In S. Thernstrom (Ed.) **Harvard encyclopedia of racial ethnic groups.** Cambridge, MA: Belknap Press of Harvard University.

CHAPTER EIGHT

A Native American Perspective

REV. REAVES NAHWOOKS

*W*e search for ways to enrich the spiritual insight of our many tribal people. The gift of our knowledge and wisdom are of those deep expressions that tend to share what life is all about. As we live and study, we learn that Western society has grown to have a very stereotypical view of Native American Indians. A good indicator is to ask any three- or four-year-old, "What is an Indian?" Even older children have strong misconceptions of the group that is thought by many people in this country to have vanished. The response usually will be hollering while patting hand over the mouth, raising two fingers over the back of the head, or raising one's hand and saying "How," as if it is significant. It is amazing in this day that this type of thinking prevails in our society. It is brought about by many reasons, among which is the attempted annihilation, assimilation, or elimination that has taken place throughout history. As a result, many people think of Native American Indians as second-class primarily because they think and act differently.

The 1990 census shows there are 1.9 million Native American Indian people in this country. That is one-half of one percent of our country's population. Even though this number is small, the influence of history, treaties, and legal relationships and obligations by the federal government on Native American Indians makes this a prominent group that needs to be dealt with. There appears to be no attempt to understand how we can respond and coexist in this society and at this time.

There are nearly three hundred tribes in this country today. Each tribe has its own culture. Each tribe has its own language, its own history, its own customs, and its own traditions, and in most cases, each tribe has different food, clothing, and shelter. Today, this has changed considerably because the influence of Western thinking has strongly changed what formerly was tradition among the Native American Indian people. Though many tribes are similar in language, dress, and food, for the most part they are different. With the many changes that have taken place historically, we take a contemporary approach to our way of life. In other words, not many things that Native American Indians do today are untouched by the Western influence. As a result, tribal cultures are not necessarily pure because of these changes. Therefore, our lives reflect a state of transition and assimilation or some form of defense or rejection of these influences. This does not affect the value of our sharing. Over the years, however, the sharing process has been exploited to one's personal benefit at the expense of Indian people. This happens in the stories and other types of writing that non-Indians claim and make a living or accumulate money from as a part of their success.

In our need to survive, we have by design and by experience incorporated alien elements of Western thought into our culture and expression. For example, we dress as other Americans, we eat similar foods, and only eat traditional foods at times like celebrations or special occasions. We speak the English language as a main source of communication because non-Indians are not able to communicate in our language unless they have lived in and learned the language of a tribe.

Today, as we try to learn about each other, emphasis is placed on slogans designed to bring us together as people — "Unity Through Diversity," "Patterns of Faith," "We Are One," and "A World Together." This is important to pursue, but we must consider some basic differences to get closer to understanding each other. We start with a number of differences that will test each of us.

First, we do not speak the same language. I am speaking in two perspectives when I refer to this area of difference. We have our tribal languages which signify words that, in some cases, are difficult to translate into other languages. Therefore, we may use adjectives inadequately in an attempt to capture the spirit of our languages. The tribal languages are so different that we have the same difficulties understanding each other's tribal language that other nationalities have understanding foreign languages. Languages are classified by anthropologists and linguists into language groups, but as a rule, Native American Indian people do not necessarily speak and understand each other.

Second, there are differences in the meaning of the words we use: for example, words like family, power, wealth, etc. "Family" in the Native American system of thinking includes the immediate family and the aunts, uncles, cousins, and even close friends as well. Cousins are acknowledged as brothers and sisters. Grandparents are thought of in the same way as a mother and father because they fill those roles as well, and in many cases, live with or close to the family.

"Power," according to Webster's dictionary, has 12 to 15 definitions. Basically, power is the ability to do something: vigor, energy, strength, property, control, influence, or authority defined by law. In math, it is the product of a number multiplied by itself. Power could also be mechanical or electrical energy as opposed to hand labor, the magnifying capacity of a lens, or an electrical supply, etc. In contrast, when tribal people refer to power, they are relating specifically to healing, medicine, and the supernatural. However, the supernatural is related only in the sense of identifying for non-Indians something beyond ordinary. Among Native American Indians, things are considered natural, rather than supernatural, because there is no such thing as the "supernatural"; it is a natural event or function that is possible. In this context, spirituality becomes important because what is spiritual and natural among tribal people may be identified as supernatural among others.

Third, "wealth," according to the dictionary, refers to riches, possession of riches, or a great quantity of anything. It also is measured in terms of money or anything that can be converted to money. On the other hand, tribal people consider wealth to be a large family. A person who has no family and dies is considered to have died poor, even though he may have an abundance of money, land, and material possessions. Richness comes from the fact that the entire family can benefit from the assets of each member of the family. Each member has a special talent, a special gift, that is important and vital to the family so that when there is a need, the entire family may respond. It also reasons that there is no need for support systems because the support systems are built into the family. Therefore, there is no need for Social Security, nursing homes, orphanages, elderly care homes, etc., because the family cares for its needs or has appropriate resources to use. In this way, wealth is present.

This difference in perceptions or beliefs form value systems that are different. One of the differences worth mentioning is that the tribal systems recognize age as important because of the wisdom that comes with age. Knowledge can be acquired by reading books or studying and asking persons who have knowledge, but wisdom comes through experiences and time in order to place values and important parts of one's life into a right relationship. In Western thinking, youth is emphasized because young people are the future leaders and will be important in the world ahead. Both are true and necessary, but they represent a difference in thinking and approach.

Another important value is the contribution to the group for the common good of the family as well as the tribe. Contribution is the ideal rather than personal recognition. In Western thinking, the emphasis is on competition and being ahead of the next person. This is reflected in the individualism of our country with each person's desire to be Number One! Giving and sharing is the mode of tribal people, in contrast to the taking and saving of Western thinking. Among Indian people, listening is a skill and is important to the personality of an Indian person. To the non-Indian, verbal expression or the ability to talk and be heard is a skill that seems to be most important. Among Native American Indians, religion is a way of life and is manifested in all that we do. It cannot be separated from life itself. In other words, Indian people attempt to live their religion. Among Western societies, religion is a segment of life that can be separated and met at certain times of the week or year; it does not conflict with other segments of life. Among tribal people, the goal is harmony with nature so that we recognize the rhythm of God's natural laws and use them and move in concert with them. Western thinking strives at mastery over nature, and therefore, is able to change things with hothouses, steroids, changing the atmosphere, and changing the cycles of life, many times using pesticides and toxins in the process.

There are many more differences that will require study and can come about with communication and more sharing. As we briefly compare these differences, it presents a real dilemma for Native American Indians because it means we must select one way of thinking over another and historically we have refused to do so. Therefore, we are faced with balancing a different cultural thinking in our lifestyle. If we select one, then we reject the other. This is not the best solution.

I am reminded of a quote by Chief Dan George, Chief of the Salish in Canada. He was one of our wisdomkeepers:

"Oh God! Like the Thunderbird of old, I shall rise again out of the sea! I shall grab instruments of the white man's success — his education, his skills, and with these new tools I shall build my race into the proudest segment of your society. Before I follow the great chiefs who have gone before us I shall see these things come to pass."

Jim Wallis, director of Sojourner's, said in October 1991:

"The real issue is the social paradigm and economic order that the Columbus event set into motion and the fact that it has dominated all our lives and in particular the lives of marginalized people for the past 500 years. There is, in fact, no new world order; we are still being governed by the old one whose economic, political, philosophical, environmental, and especially spiritual roots can be traced back to the conquest and colonization of America."

We are all a part of that time whether we like it or not. We have heard of the vanishing people; we have heard of the birth of the slave trade; we have heard of the endangered land and peoples; we have heard of tyranny and poverty and illness and dominance. So the conquest is not over. The warfare in this country and the world is still taking place. The destruction of a way of life (cultures) is taking place. Each of us is a part of this society, so we must try or begin to understand each other and how people who are different think and feel. What is happening in the world affects not just one, but everyone in this country. We must look to alternatives to reconcile and renew our lives and existence. We must eliminate paternalism, subordination of people who are different, dominance by those who have power, and we must generate an understanding of cultures that influence viewpoints. We live in chaos that requires different approaches to and affirmations of each other and with new commitments that will make our world a better world to live in.

We must create better relationships. It is my thinking that we must create a "Right Relationship" between ourselves and God, a "Right Relationship" between ourselves and other people (humanity), and a "Right Relationship" between ourselves and Nature. No one can tell us what that "Right Relationship" is, but we recognize and know it when it comes to us. When we are alienated from God, we suffer tension, anxiety, and lack of purpose. When we get close to God, we experience a better relationship and joy and comfort and confidence. Coming closer to these ideal relationships will result in balance and harmony, and this is what I term as Peace.

We must live in this world together. Therefore, we must deal with better understanding of each other so we can exist in happiness. We can live together in Peace or die together.

The REV. REAVES NAHWOOKS is the pastor and developer of the Indian Community Church in Lincoln and Omaha, Nebraska. He was ordained by the Rainy Mountain Indian Church in Mount View, Oklahoma, and holds a doctorate in ministry from Colgate Rochester Divinity School. In addition, he has 35 years experience in policy development and program administration with the federal, Native American, and civil rights programs. His essay in this volume was first presented at the 1993 symposium, "Fostering Spiritual Growth Among At-Risk Youth: Multicultural Perspectives."

From Theory to Practice

CHAPTER NINE

Effective Strategies for Working with At-Risk Youth

DR. LORRAINE MONROE

I am going to talk about effective strategies for working with at-risk youth. But I call them strategies that transform children's lives. Strategies that interrupt the cycle of poverty and despair. Strategies that allow us to do the worthiest work.

I've taught for a long time. I taught English in junior high school and high school both in Harlem and in the Bronx in New York City. I've been a New York City person since I was a month and a half old and have lived almost in the same vicinity my entire life.

If you were to look at all of those statistics about what makes kids at risk, I was an at-risk child. And that is why I know that the work that I have done and the work that you are doing is the only work. I would not be here without people such as yourselves, who interrupted the cycle.

Part of my background is that I am a child of teenage parents. I am a child of parents who didn't finish high school. I am a child of parents who worked dead-end jobs with no future. I am a child of a broken home, a child who lived in surroundings (a four-room slum apartment) that were not conducive "to the world at large" for achieving anything.

And yet today I have five degrees and am able to go across the country and talk about not only my background but also the work that I've done. It's because of people such as yourselves. It's also because of my parents. Although they stopped loving each other, they never stopped loving me.

That background is something that I never, never forget. I go around the country and people ask me, "What are we going to do with these black children, brown children, red children? What are we going to do with these hillbilly white kids who come out of the Kentucky hills?" I answer back, "Teach them. Be with them. Be for them."

And overriding all of that is to remember yourself. Some of the people who are helping kids were at risk themselves. Some of us get into these jobs simply because we realize the blessings that we've had and we want to give something back. We did not all spring full blown into being able to help people. We had shattering things happen to us, and we overcame those things. That ought to not only inform our heads, but also inform our hearts, when we work with children who are at risk.

You also need to know that I backed into becoming a teacher. I was going to be a doctor because I thought a doctor is a person who can make a difference. If something's rotten, you cut it out. If something's broken, you put a cast on it. If something's cut, you sew it up. And then you can see what you have done.

However, when you teach, when you do service jobs with kids, you are working in blind faith. You are not always sure of what you are doing and whether it has efficacy. And yet you work on.

And so I said I wanted to be a doctor. I was in Hunter College. I was a junior. And my counselor — it was the first and last time I ever saw my counselor in college — called me down and showed me my cumulative record and said, "Do you want to go to medical school?" I said, "Sure." She said, "You are not passing Quantitative Analysis, Qualitative Analysis, Analytical Geometry, Trig. What medical school is going to take you?" I said, "I don't know." I think I was about 17 1/2. She said, "Well look, I see you're getting straight A's in English. Why don't you become an English teacher?" I said, "Okay," and now I am an English teacher.

156

When you get to be a little older and you look back on your life, you find out that you're really not in charge of your life. Sometimes you're lucky enough to do what you're sent to do. The African bushmen say, "There is a dream dreaming you." And when you hit it right, you do the dream.

So here was this counselor looking at what I thought was my dream. But God had another plan. He said, "Go teach." And so I started teaching and found that I was absolutely awful in the beginning. Awful. And, I thought, "Seventh-grade girls. Where did they come from?" It took me a while to understand some things about those girls and, at the same time, understand some things about myself. That's the dual work of working with at-risk kids. It's not just understanding them. It's understanding yourself, too.

Ultimately I became a really good teacher. I taught for 17 years in schools in different parts of New York City. And then I became an administrator.

I had the experience of working under people who had no vision. Never mind the skills — they had no vision of what to do with poor children.

And then I was lucky enough to work under an incredible administrator who had vision. I learned to be an administrator from him (although I didn't really want to be an administrator).

Ultimately, I became a principal. I was called on August 26th to become principal on August 27th. Anybody who knows anything about schools and administration will know that something must be wrong with an institution if the head of it calls three days before it is to open and says he's not coming back. So I was absolutely dazed. I didn't say, "Why is the other principal leaving so suddenly?" I didn't say, "Where is the school?" I didn't say, "What kind of school is it?" I just said, "Yes."

I guess I'm kind of a testimony that you absolutely cannot outrun your fate. Absolutely cannot. So I said, "Okay. Sure."

It was a school in deep, deep trouble. It was a school in the South Bronx. It was a school that was 48 percent black, 48 percent Latino, 2 percent I-don't-know, and one white boy who thought he was black.

So I began the work. I had to remember my background, a background very similar to what these children had. And I knew it was possible. I knew it was possible to make a difference in their lives if the staff and I put it together right.

You have to also understand that kids who are at risk don't want to be at risk. They really do want to escape. They really want to do better. I don't want to sound simplistic and say it's as easy as one, two, three, and it all happens. But I do want to say that if you find some fundamental truths and you continue to teach those truths and are persistent with them, you can turn children around. We worked very hard and did that. And then I moved on to do other things.

So let me now tell you a bit about some of the strategies I used in doing what I call the "worthiest" work — the work of transforming children's lives. And let me suggest that we begin with an examination of ourselves. You can't turn anybody else around unless you examine your own motives for doing the work and for being the way you are. Ask yourself, "Why am I here with these youth? What do I hope to accomplish?" We need to examine our own humanity and know what our strengths are and what our weaknesses are, what turns us off, and what makes us awful with children.

I used to be girls' dean. That is a euphemism for working with bad girls. It was again one of those things that happened to me in passing. I was walking through the cafeteria and the assistant principal and his friend were sitting there and they asked me to come over. I said, "What?" They said, "You want to be the girls' dean?" I said, "It sounds good. What is it?" They replied, "You just work with some of the girls who are in trouble." And I said, "Okay."

It was again one of those things I had backed into. I was girls' dean and I thought I was good. You know one of the things that happens when you do this work for a long time? You think you are terrific. Bring on Godzilla. Bring on King Kong. But God will send somebody your way to make you humble. And sure enough, up the path came this girl. That was a time in the South Bronx when we had gangs; kids wearing colors, nail heads and hobnail boots, and jackets with monkey skin hanging off. I mean, terrifying looking.

158

Well, there was this girl who came into my life. I can remember she was like the first "bad girl" I had in the seventh-grade. There was something in her spirit that totally clashed with my spirit. Now, that's something you have to come to recognize when you're a servant person. You can't rescue everybody. But your ego says you can. What happened was that I started operating outside of myself. Whenever I saw this girl, I would write her up for picky little stupid things — standing in the hall, chewing gum on the staircase, being in the bathroom too long. I mean it really got to be that picayune. But she was ultimately irritating other people and she was suspended. And at the suspension hearing, this very humane principal brought everybody who dealt with this girl together so the parent would have the whole picture. Everybody went around and said that everything they tried with this girl hadn't worked. And I had my folder there; I'm usually very organized. I opened up the folder. Papers flew out because I was writing this kid up on napkins, pieces of toilet paper, whatever I could get my hands on at the moment. I started getting into a real frantic talk about the kid. And the principal was looking at me strangely because that's not how I usually operated. When the hearing was over, he asked me what was wrong. I said, "I don't know but this kid really gets to me." He told me to calm down. "You are good," he said. "But understand you are not the one for this child. Somebody else on staff is the one for this child."

So we've talked about strategies. One of the first strategies is knowing ourselves. And knowing when to let go of a person and being able to say, "Somebody else in this place is the one for this child" without losing ego. I am glad that child was in my life so I would learn that.

I also think we need to examine our expectations of kids. We should make them high, but not so high that they're unreachable. And we need to attend to environment. I now do coaching in a program that I started called "The Center for Minority Achievement." We're working in six intermediate and junior high schools in Manhattan. Understand that reform cannot be imposed from above; you reform each particular site according to each particular site's needs.

I'm doing some coaching of new teachers, old teachers, and principals, or whatever the principal wants me to do. In this one particular place, a teacher I once helped get through her first year asked me to help a teacher who was struggling.

They had put this new teacher in the basement. She was in a room where — I am not kidding — 75 percent of the lights in the ceiling were not working. There was filth on the floor. The bulletin boards were a wreck. I sat in the back of the room. She had said it would be all right for me to observe her. So I made copious notes. There was absolutely no consciousness on the part of this person of how environment speaks to children. And at times when you, the teacher, are not speaking, the environment is speaking. Kids who are at risk could come from places that are shattered and fractured. You should not think that your ego is so great that the students are totally fascinated with you whenever you are talking. Therefore, the walls should speak your truth. There should be stuff on the wall that inspires, that says, "You are capable." The walls should say, "Welcome. We want good things to happen to you."

I told her that there were a couple of things I wanted her to do. I said I would come back on Monday and we would talk more. As I was walking out of the room, I stopped and went back and asked her for her phone number and said I would call her that night. I walked out and said to myself, "No other class can come in that room with it looking like that."

So I ran up to the principal and custodian and asked about fixing the lights. I said, "Give me a broom. Give me some construction paper. Give me a stapler. Give me some kids." In 20 minutes, we had cleaned the floor. We had redone the bulletin board. I told the teacher to straighten her desk so that when children came, they had a sense of order and stability.

This was brand new to her. I wondered about the institutions that train our people who serve children and do not address this fundamental idea of an ordered, welcoming environment.

Children can pick up when you think of them as "different." And different means "bad." The children are different from you in lots of ways and that becomes the fabric of how you deal with them. If you are condescending to them by the language and behavior you use and the attitude you have, you will never be effective with them. I've been in rooms where teachers never touch the children. They never sit next to their students. They never move beyond the invisible line that separates their desk from the students. Those of you who have observed schools will know that I am not lying. How can a teacher, or any serving person, say, "I honor you. I am here for you. But I will never touch you. I will never sit next to you. I will never stroke you. I will only poke you."

That's the kind of self-examination that we have to have. We need expectations that never say "Preposterous" when a kid tells you his or her dream.

I've developed a phrase that I call "conscious teaching." Conscious teaching means that I say, right out of the chute, exactly what I'm expecting out of the session with the kids, exactly what I'm expecting of the people that I train or talk to.

Those things are crucial. Finally, before I get to the concrete strategies, you have to use memory. When I train people to work with at-risk youth, I say, "I want you to write on a piece of paper what you were like at the age of these children. Write at the top of the page the age of the children you work with. Take five minutes to write down what you were like at that age. I've had people say, "Don't make me do that because it's painful." Nobody wants to remember how he or she was at age 13 or 14 years old because it was, even in the best of circumstances, traumatic.

It's hard to remember that pain. You don't remember how your voice squeaked as a young man. And how embarrassing that was when the teacher called on you and your voice would go up and down when you had to speak. It was painful when you didn't grow, and the other boys were growing. Or, when other girls were getting breasts and you weren't getting them. I had a teasing father and he sure didn't help my self-image much.

161

Cruelty. Right? Cruelty. When you don't get your period and all the other girls are getting their periods and talking about them. And then you lied about it, too. Or, boys lie about stuff that happened when it really didn't.

If you're going to be a good worker with kids, you have to remember what being a kid is like. You have to remember what their concerns are. Good teachers play to the concerns. Good workers acknowledge, "Yeah, this is crazy time for you. I know it's a crazy time for you. But others have done the crazy time and successfully moved on in their lives. So we're going to take care of that in whatever ways you want to. We're going to do my work, too. Cause I'm the grownup in the situation."

Those of us who are very effective with kids never let go of being the grownup in the situation. The people who fail with kids not only remember what they were like when they were kids, but also think that the way to help youth is to act like them. Kids don't respect that. They laugh at it. But they very much respect the person who knows and who remembers and who is always the adult in the situation. Let me tell you some of the things that will give you that kind of groundwork.

I think, number one, you need to examine what I call the "ethos belief" or "mission statement" of the place and continue examining it. Boys Town does it well. You come up the drive and you see a statue of a kid with another kid on his shoulders and the slogan says, "He ain't heavy, Father... He's m' brother."

Any institution worth its salt, any service worth its salt, any classroom worth its salt, ought to have a mission that's brief, that says it all, and that everybody knows.

My second recommendation is that there should be some forthright training of people who work with kids and at-risk youth. They need to know the developmental stage of the children they're serving. You cannot assume that when people come in to work with four- and five-year-olds they know what a four- and five-year-old is like developmentally. With adolescents, you know what normal teenage behavior is, too. You have to talk about the significance of the noncognitive part of what you're doing. When I became a teacher, I thought, "Well, I'll teach the classics like Shakespeare and that will take care of the cognitive part of these children and they will just go out in the world and do well."

The more I got into my work, the more I knew that this idea was not right. We have to take care of the total child.

Why do we lose children in droves? Because people don't look at the whole kid. They don't know about their development. They don't know that there are other needs to be attended to. It's the head and it's the heart and it's the body. All of these have to be attended to.

People have to be trained for that. You don't just teach a "subject." You have to attend to the whole person sitting in front of you. That's the kind of training we have to have so that people not only know their stuff but also the significance of their language, their behavior, their expectations, and their attitudes when dealing with young people.

You want to help people? You have to have some non-negotiable rules. You have to have simple rules and regulations. That's crucial for kids who are at risk because part of what they're suffering from is a lack of stable things in their lives that say, "These are some truths." We need to set rules and regulations that allow us to live in civility and to take care of each other. Those are wonderful sessions when staff members get together and agree on non-negotiable rules to help the children.

If we're going to rescue our kids, we've got to do some different things. When I was principal, one of the things I realized was that if you're going to turn children around, you've got to stop doing "the same old, same old." Especially for the kids who are at risk. They always come in at the beginning of the new year and say, "I bet she's going to do the same old stuff she did last year." Some of the same old stuff is good, so you hang on to it. But some of it is not good, so drop it and invent some new stuff.

I am very much for innovation and creativity, as long as you have a plan. Ask the kids questions like, "How do I get my electricity turned back on? How do I negotiate the red tape from my welfare check?" Ask them all kinds of questions like that. Then have the kids do research and bring the answers back to you.

Enlist the help of other people to do different things for kids who are at risk. Take the kids out of the building. Allow them to know the larger world and the larger world to know them so that they know what opportunities are out there. Build as much flexibility into the plan as you can.

Another strategy we used was to conduct a survey of students' and teachers' talents and interests and needs and wants and lacks, and then build a program around that. It's one of those simple, elegant things. How do you help people? You ask them what they need and what they're good at.

No child is a failure in every aspect of his or her life. If you want to rescue that child, you have to do a survey or find some way to ask, "If you weren't here, what would you be doing? If it didn't count for grades, what would you love to learn? If nobody mocks you, what would you like to do?"

And kids will tell you. What they tell you is the point of rescue.

Another thing that we did was increase the experience and exposure to the creative arts. Children are not rescued by quadratic equations. It's a rare human being that says, "You know why I stand here before you a successful person? It was a quadratic equation." It's usually a person, an event, a trip that opened the kid up and out to say, "Wow! People do that? And get money? This is the way you walk through the world? This is the way of doing...." And they don't know these things if we keep them in our institutions. You have to get some successful people who relate to the children into the building. You have to get people who once were in those difficult situations to come and talk to children and say: "I am a living example of a person who had this kind of shattered home and background, and here is how I got out."

Allow the person to talk about failure. Many kids think successful people were born successful and that they never had a problem. You need people who use honest and discreet self-revelation. Let

164

them tell the kids that they once failed at something and that they picked themselves up and kept on going.

Tell kids about life. No one has a totally successful life. Tell kids that when they try, they're going to fail even when they're most successful. But the really successful people keep on keeping on. Conscious teaching and training says that to children. Tell kids they will fail. Tell them to never give up. There will be failures and successes throughout their lives. But don't give up!

Talk to kids about life lines and then help them dream the line. Tell them to write about their lives from when they were born to the present and put all those big events in it. Then tell them to dream their lives from now until they are 21. Ask them what they want in that life line. Then sit down and have some sessions with them on how they plan to make the rest of the dream life line work. And then ask them how you can help them realize their dreams.

When children leave us, they need some continuity. Don't assume that they're just going to keep on keeping on without support. You've got to network them back to you and make that a set procedure. Tell them that at certain times you want them to see you or that you're going to call them up to find out how it's going. Or you network them to somebody else who will do that. People who are at risk are at risk because they don't have coping mechanisms; they need support and encouragement. That's why we're in this work; we're the ones who keep them going.

Talk to children about their "last personal best." My son is a track star and I learned that expression from him. Those of you who coach know that. When you're training people who are at risk, they assume you want them to go from zero to a hundred in a leap — from failing to superb. If you're going to rescue people who have chronic failure in their lives, you have to work in increments.

I'm asking you to look at their last personal best. Tell kids that you want them to improve and be better each time. If you're going to help people who are at risk, you've got to say to them: "I know where you are. I see how you're moving. Let's analyze how you're making this progress." It's not that the youth is going to get 100 percent better, because for people who have failed, that's an impossibility. It's finding out how the youth can be better next time. It's finding out how you can help the youth do better.

How do we use other children in the process of helping at-risk children? We bring back kids we had under our tutelage and we say: "Talk to these children. Tell them." Children can counsel and peer tutor each other, too. There's power in that because they will reveal stuff to their peers that they wouldn't reveal to you. You just have to sit back quietly, train somebody well, and watch them run.

How many times do we withhold praise because what a child did isn't exactly what we wanted? And yet the kid is giving us as much as he can give. I'm not talking about giving things and having pizza parties. I'm talking about a word of praise that can stay in a kid's head forever. We need to train people to develop 20 praise statements that they can say to children; statements like, "That's good. I see improvement. This is better."

Frequent praise for children who are at risk for multiple reasons is powerful. Being with them is powerful. Touching them is powerful.

There are some people who work among us called coaches. Coaches have power over at-risk children that some of us don't have. We need to look at the power coaches have. My son's coach would tell him, "I want you to suit up." This is the middle of January. "Suit up in blue shorts. Come out to the park and do 50 laps through the park and then give me 50 push-ups." I had a hard time getting my son to take out the garbage, but yet the coach had him running laps in the dead of winter!

We need to find those people who have that kind of power over children and do some training. Say, "Listen coach. While you're coaching, could you tell the kids that some of the stuff you're doing with them is transferable to other parts of their lives? That they didn't learn how to do a layup by doing one layup and quitting. That it was perseverance that paid off. And that perseverance can transfer to other parts of learning. When you have a good team effort, tell them a good team effort works in other aspects of their lives."

166

We work in the dark and we work in faith. But we work to interrupt the cycle of poverty and despair. It is the worthiest work of all. I can tell you stories about children I've taught in Central Harlem over the years about whom I thought nothing good would come.

You have to know yourself well enough to say, "I will do the thing for these children that I love. I will expose them to the passion of my intellectual life." I loved poetry as an English teacher. You have to only say that to children — "Now we're going to do poems" — and it's universal groans. I say, "I don't care. Because I love poetry and when I finish, you're going to love it too." That's the conviction of the passionate adult. Kids ought to know why you love chemistry. You ought to be going wacky about chemistry if that's your subject. They ought to know, if you're doing religious education, that this is the only subject in the world. They will say, "Why, there must be something to this religious education. Look how crazy he is about it."

So I'm doing Shakespeare's sonnets with a class of seventh-graders. I told them that they were going to memorize a sonnet and recite it in front of the class. I told them they could learn song lyrics to 45 rap songs; all I'm asking for is 14 lines. I told them they could choose their own sonnet. I believe that when you're working with kids who are at risk, you need to give them alternatives. There's a whole list of things you can do and, of course, you select the topics so that every single topic means that they have to stretch themselves.

The day came to recite the sonnets. There was an incredibly bright kid in class but he never showed how intelligent he was.

I didn't call on him first. I let about five kids go and then I asked him to recite. He starts off and he stumbles. And I feed him a line and he stumbles. And I feed him another line and he stumbles. I say, "Okay, you can take your seat now." He sits down and I feel bad about the whole situation. When the term ended, I gave him a 75. I didn't see him for 15 to 17 years. Then one day, I'm walking through my block and there he was. He said, "Ms. Monroe. You remember me?" I said I did. He said, "Do you remember when we

167

did those sonnets in class?" I said sure. He said, "You thought I wasn't listening, right?" I said, "You gave every evidence that you weren't." He said, "No, I was listening. I was giving you everything I could. There was so much trouble at home with my mother and father and grandmother. I gave you all I could give you at that time. But I remember." I said, "Really?" He said, "Shall I compare thee to a summer's day? Thou art more lovely and more temperate." He did the whole sonnet perfectly. I said, "Wow!"

I'm in the street and I'm ecstatic. People had to wonder what was wrong with me. I'm getting goose pimples. I asked what he was doing. He said, "I write the back page of *Time* magazine."

I couldn't believe it! When I got home I ran upstairs and found *Time* magazine. Sure enough. Back page. There he was. And I said, "See. That's why we've got to be fine every time. That's why we have to look at what we're doing and say, 'I'm not giving up on excellence. I'm not giving up on quality. I may give options. But I know what is right. I am holding on to my truth. I'm going to do it, because I know in the end it's going to be good.'" That's the way we work with kids.

I would like to close by mentioning an article that I read. About a year or so ago, a man did a study of children who came from homes of alcoholics and abusive parents and schizophrenic parents. And these children all succeeded in school. And in life. The man said he had to talk to these children to find out what it was that allowed them to escape.

The children he interviewed said two things. First, they said they knew it was crazy at home. But they found somebody else to substitute for the crazy parent. They went to school. They went to a center. They found another significant adult. The second thing they said was that they found a thing to do that they loved. They could encapsulate themselves in it to block out all the noise and the confusion.

So the charge I leave with you is that each of you must believe that you are the one for children who are at risk. Do whatever is in your power to rescue the child. Encapsulate him or her with passion and competencies so he or she can escape and become a free-stand-ing, economically independent, contributing member of society. We all ask God's help and blessings in this work.

> *DR. LORRAINE MONROE is a nationally known public educator in residence at Bank Street College of Education in New York City. She is founder of the Center for Minority Achievement and a national consultant for Effective Education and Administration for Poor and At-Risk Youth. In addition, she brings a wealth of experience as a teacher and principal to her contribution to this volume. Her essay was first presented at the 1989 symposium, "Teaching Moral Values to At-Risk Youth."*

CHAPTER TEN

Setting At-Risk Youth Free Through Spiritual Growth

REV. BRUCE WALL

n 1967 I was standing on my porch in the Dorchester section of Boston. I was talking to one of my street buddies. There were 13 of us. We thought we were "bad" dudes. I was talking to John. (John went on to find himself involved in a life of crime.) But that day, he was pointing his finger at me. It was August, it was hot, and he was saying, "Bruce, out of all of us, you're the one that's hanging in at that church and you're the one who's listening to that preacher. Go ahead and make it on behalf of all of us."

All of my boys were making their decisions. Some became Black Muslims. Some became Black Panthers. Many were incarcerated. But John said, "Bruce, go ahead and make it on behalf of all of us." And about three weeks after that discussion, as a matter of fact, I walked into my bedroom and I got on my knees and I committed my life to Jesus Christ. Man, while I was on my knees I remembered everything the preacher had preached. I didn't understand it but I understood something about giving your heart to Jesus. That afternoon I gave my life over to God. Three weeks later, my pastor took this high-risk teenager and sent me to a predominantly white Christian college campus in the Berkshire Mountains near Lennox, Massachusetts. Three-quarters of the students at Berkshire were white and from the South. Many said they'd never gone to school with a person of color before. The students asked me questions like,

"Does it rub off?" and "Is it true that you once had tails?" One student who wanted to be a missionary to Africa put a note on my door: "Boom, boom, boom. Darkie go back to Africa." That really hurt. But a white student from New Hampshire came by and put his arms around me, and God used him to carry me through four years of Berkshire Christian College. Four years later I graduated!

Then I walked into the seminary at Gordon Conwell Theological Seminary and I graduated! That was miracle one. Miracle two was when God opened the door for me to be a clerk/magistrate in the juvenile justice system — the same juvenile justice system that I could have ended up in on the other side of the bench. That same year, God also opened the door for me to return to my home church, the Twelfth Baptist Church in Roxbury, the same church where Dr. Martin Luther King Jr. served when he was attending Boston University. I was called to be the youth pastor to the same group of young people I belonged to years before, rebelling and trying to lead them out of the church. So I've been around.

Youth who lived in America in 1967 were going through a cultural kind of political crisis — the war in Vietnam, the black revolution in America. I was in the street shouting "I'm black and I'm proud." I was articulating and I believed it. I was into the civil rights movement and there was racial unrest all over the country. But in 1967 there was a moral crisis much different from the one we're facing today. Today, this youth moral crisis can start in our homes, communities, or ministries. I want to submit that young people who don't have a strong spiritual foundation that is grounded in God are in for a tough, tough ride in the Nineties. Make no bones about it.

Our youth and our families, in my opinion, have been targeted for defeat. There's a sign that I have downtown in Juvenile Court and it says, "Wanted Dead or Alive." I have my name on it. "Wanted Dead or Alive." I try to remind myself daily that Satan wants me spiritually dead and dysfunctional. There is an evil satanic force that wants our kids. Satan wants our children dead or alive — preferably dead.

I also have a wall we erected last year. Last year, it had the names of 61 teenagers who have died in the black community over the past five years through violence. Sixty-one. Today there are 82 names on that wall. Tomorrow when I go home for a march in Boston, I have to add 40 more names of kids who have died in the community. Wanted dead or alive... preferably dead.

I knew a young man by the name of Roy Allen. One day I was teaching a Sunday school class and this teenager came in; he walked in kind of sheepishly. He had his hat tipped to the side and had his Walkman on. It was 9:30 in the morning. It was cold. He came into the Sunday school class and I said, "Hey, dude. What are you doing? Come on in." He said, "Well, okay. I'll come in for a while." What I didn't know was that the owner of the local skating rink was sentencing children who got in trouble on the skating floor to my Sunday school class. Roy came in and said, "Okay, I'll have to come to four of these."

I said, "Come on in man. You stay for 10 minutes and I'll say you were here for the whole session. Just come on in." My "man" came in and sat down. We were reading the Scripture and asking questions. Roy came for four classes, five, six, seven, eight, nine, ten, eleven, twelve. Then one day I opened the *Boston Globe* and there in the paper I saw the name of a teenager — the first teenager in the Boston Public School System to die right on the classroom floor. He was knifed. His name was Kingsley. I looked at the picture. It was Roy. Man, it hurt. And I wanted to cry.

But I said, "Bruce, if you cry for Roy, you're going to start crying for all of these kids and then you're going to become high-risk and they're going to commit you." So I didn't cry. But Roy was stabbed and Roy was involved in Sunday school. And because I didn't have enough strong men who were committed to going into the streets to work with these young people, Roy slipped back to the corner and was involved in drugs.

So those youth who are spiritually blind, in my opinion, are without a homing device, without radar, and they're vulnerable and susceptible to destruction. One of the things that I'm trying to do with young people is to find that radar, that homing device, and somehow put it inside their hearts and their minds so that whenever they're tempted to mess up or do crazy things, that homing device will somehow connect with God and they'll have strength and wisdom and insight to make the right decisions. Our kids need a homing device.

In secular terms, I want to raise young people and help them live in this doomed society. Just because the society is doomed doesn't mean that our kids have to live doomed and act doomed and walk doomed. I want to teach young people how to live abundant lives. When you see teenagers you work with, you walk up to them and say, "How you doing? What's happening?"

They say, "Everything's okay. I'm hangin' in. I'm surviving." I'm teaching kids not to say that. I tell them, "If you slap me five, high five or low five, tell me that you're living abundantly." Try to teach kids how to live abundantly, not just to survive.

I think that we need to be like the Old Testament biblical character, Nehemiah. He struggled to rebuild walls. I'm trying to rebuild the wall of protection around the youth I love and the youth I work with. We need a holistic approach to reaching young people. I think some churches make mistakes. I think some of us make mistakes in the church. We say we've got to get them saved. We count up how many we got saved and then we walk away from them. Those of us who are working in the clinical field talk to a young person. The young person's eyes are bright. We've made a difference and sometimes, we walk away.

I want a holistic approach, an approach where you reach young people spiritually and wake them up, then stay with them. I want some of us to commit our lives to the young people whom we are working with. I'm 41 years of age. I committed my life to God when I was 18. My pastor met me in the streets when I was 13. My pastor is still monitoring me, still hanging in with me. And I pray that he's going to hang in with my son.

Who's got a holistic approach? I want to help young people, not only in the Sunday school but also when they leave the Sunday school. We've got 40 kids now. We're touching them, we're loving them, we're holding them, we're caring for them. But then I'm sending them back home. I don't have a Boys Town. When I send them back home, they come back to me the next Sunday broken. Why? Because many of their issues stem from their homes.

One of my workers said we need to start walking to each child's home after Sunday school. Walk into the home and get a feel of what is happening and then treat the homes. I don't know how we're going to achieve this optimistic goal. But that's what we're going to do.

We need to coat the minds and the hearts of young people with what I'm calling "spiritual Maalox." We need to coat the minds and the hearts of kids, whether you call them high-risk kids, no-risk kids, or whatever. We must coat their minds with the very presence of who God is. I submit to you that you're going to find young people who are going to be able to at least be stabilized so that you can begin to talk with them and deal with them. Because until I'm able to stabilize the young folks I'm working with, I can't reach them. I'll give you some examples.

In Massachusetts, the juvenile justice system, the State Department of Social Services, and the public school systems just don't understand that young people need a belief system. I contend that the belief system needs to be biblically based. Too many youth are spiritually alive to a satanic presence in their lives. My goal is to replace the negative belief system with one that will inspire youth to live for what is right and wholesome.

In two weeks we're going to call an amnesty in Boston. We'll put a yellow ribbon around the Chez Vous Rollerway logo and ask the mothers and kids to turn in their weapons. We are going to march with them. I want to arm the young people. But I don't want to arm them with weapons. I want to arm them with the armor of God.

Now you'll have to come to Bruce Wall's Religion Class 101 for me to define what that is. But unless young people are rooted in a faith, rooted in a relationship with God, they will succumb to drugs, teenage pregnancies, suicide, alcohol, drugs, and Satan worship. If you're part of their religious belief system, that's what you're going to do. We've got to group them and ground them in a faith in God. It's got to be biblical.

This is the most powerful thing I've said to some of my young people: "God has a plan for your life." First, that's powerful all by itself. My pastor believed in me; I did not believe in myself. But I believed that if my pastor believed in me, I could not let him down and I must be somebody. As I grew, I transferred that to God and then I became somebody in my own right. There was a process.

So I tell kids, "Hey dude. Hey sister. God has a plan for your life. And you need to discover that plan. You need to search it out and find it."

I say to young people, "You were not hatched." You may not understand this and I don't know if you're a creationist or an evolutionist, but I want to tell you that some of my kids act like animals because they've been told that's where they came from. So I'm a creationist. I tell kids that they were created by a living God. And you should see the change and gleam in the eyes of these young people when I share that: "God has a plan for you. You need to find it. And you were created for a purpose, dude."

So my kids now have meaning; they have a foundation to land their lives on. They have a little bit of hope. They have a chance and they believe in something.

Here's what I mean. I had a young teenager; her name was Jean. Her sisters' names are "Get Down" and "Lay Flat," and boy, were they tough. Jean was angry at me because I allowed two of the teenagers to put an article in our ministry's newsletter. I didn't know that was going to start a war. Jean also was angry with the other young people. Jean was going to bring her sisters to the Sunday school to destroy them and annihilate them. That Sunday they got into a little war at the skating rink. I sat down and talked with Jean and I talked with the young people and it was amazing. I said, "I thought your life was going through a process of change because you're supposed to believe in God." One young person said, "You're right." That is why they did not use weapons. My young folk were developing a conscience. They are beginning to develop a belief system. They are learning that there's a right and there's a wrong way to live.

There's a Scripture verse I want to give you. It's an Old Testament verse, Providence 22:6. It says, "Train up a child in the way we want them to go...." Train up a child the way the Department of Social Services wants, the way the judge wants, the way the clinician wants. Train up children in the way they should go and when they are old, they will not depart from that. A lot of kids depart from what we teach them as children. You can't take that truth out of their minds.

(We've been talking about inner-city kids. In case you need to be reminded, young people in the suburbs who were nurtured also can be high-risk kids.)

Chimp, a girl from Lexington, Massachusetts, said in front of 2,000 people, "I have everything. My parents have given me everything. I have all the material goods in the world. I got it all. I'm doing well. But because of the pressure of the expectations on behalf of my parents and my teachers, I have the anxiety. And I want to turn to all that stuff."

Little Jerome from Roxbury, Massachusetts, said, "I don't have all the material things in the world. I want the $100 or $200 sneakers that are made in Taiwan for $10 and I'm not going to work at McDonald's (the value structure). I'm going to work at the local corner and I'll either be a runner or a seller. I think I'll be a runner. A runner makes more." But the problem with running, he says, is that if you take the package to the door, there's a strong chance that the person might keep your package and his money and kill you. "But I'd still rather take my chance," Jerome said. "I need the money."

Now here's a question: Who is raising most of the kids in the high-risk inner-city areas and suburbs? I say the government is raising the kids. I tell parents and churches that if we diminish our influence in the lives of our kids, the Department of Social Services, the schools, the judges, the court clinicians, the police officers, the court magistrates, the probation officers, the parole officers, the court officials, and the day care workers will take over. Do you know what happens to a child when all of us converge on him or her at one time?

Individually, we might do a good job. But not all of us at one time. So we have to somehow challenge churches to say to the state, "Please, we want you out of the business of raising our families." And I'm saying to churches that they need to be raising these families.

Who's training up our children? I had a young teenager who was on the train; he was on his way home with his boys. He saw another teenager and he said, "Give it up." As I was hearing his case, I said, "What does 'Give it up' mean?" He said, "I wanted him to give up his hat, his coat, and his clothes." I said, "On the train, in broad daylight?" He said, "Yes." I said, "And what was going to happen if he didn't give it up?"

"My boy was going to shoot him."

If I granted that complaint, that child, at age 14, could be tried as an adult in Massachusetts. And if that child is tried as an adult at 14, or 15, or 16, and is incarcerated with adults, what happens? He's gone. I'm in competition with the state because I'm saying to the state that we must be involved in these young peoples' lives spiritually, even that kid who said, "Give it up." We've got to reach him.

There is a couple, a husband and wife, who are in the Department of Youth Services. They teach Bible study classes to kids who have been incarcerated by the state. Know who called them in? Some of the state officials. Know why? Because there are 50 Bible studies classes all over the state and these classes are transforming kids' lives. Now, we couldn't go public and do a story in the *Boston Globe* or the *Boston Herald* newspapers or in *Time* magazine because this couple would be thrown out. But they're teaching those classes. There's a moral crisis in the home. There's a moral crisis in the school. There's a moral crisis in the church.

I left Twelfth Baptist Church two years, three months, two days, and five hours ago. I left the organized church because I wanted to be where troubled youth congregate. I left the pulpit. At my church we had 10 pastors. My only responsibility was to work with the children. It's all I had to do. It was exciting. It's all I did. I worked as a clerk/magistrate in the court by day, and in the evenings, seven days a week, I was the youth pastor. A lot of my colleagues in the court were burning out after working with these kids for two or three years. The crimes included violent rapes and murders. We had 680 child abuse petitions last year in the juvenile courts. The year before we had 340. Eighty-five percent were drug-related. Kids were coming out of their mothers' wombs drug-addicted. My friends were burning out but I wasn't burning out. I was hanging in there. I was hanging in there only because in dealing with these young people and teaching them a belief system, some of the same kids who were failing in the courts were beginning to stand once we got them into the church. Kids who wouldn't read in school were reading for me in Sunday school class. Kids who wouldn't take tests in schools were taking tests for me in Sunday school class. And after 15 years of being the youth pastor, I decided I needed to leave, and I left. And after convincing my wife that this was a calling in my life, I tried to figure out where the kids hung out in the city of Boston.

I thought about the Chez Vous Rollerway. But I didn't want to go there because they called it Pistol City. It was tough. It was really tough. And I'm not a hero in disguise. And I am not a fool. I would prefer to have a small group of teens to work with at the Juvenile Court.

But I went to Chez Vous and we started a Sunday school class. You've got to understand that I was a youth evangelist and a court official. At church I could say, "Roll over, sit down, come to Sunday school," and they would do it. At court I could say, "Take off your hat, sit down, listen to me." But on their turf, they controlled. I didn't control. When you go on their turf, whether you're a clinician, a teacher, whatever, they're in charge. And if you don't have your own belief system, don't go.

So I said to the owner, "I want to teach a Sunday school class at your skating rink." And you know what she said? She said, "Praise the Lord. John the manager and I have been praying that somebody would come to help us out."

That was my open door. Now you need to understand that kids skate there seven days a week. I only go two days — Sunday to teach, Friday to hang out. That's all I do is hang out. On Friday nights there are 250 to 300 kids skating. I just walk in on a Friday night and say to the Lord, "How do I break this? How do I get in here?" And kids would identify me and I would back up. It was almost like trying to fish for kids to come on Sundays.

I was waiting in class the first Sunday. Man, I knew these kids were coming. I'm the court magistrate. I'm the cat at Juvenile Court. They're coming. They're coming to Sunday school. I'm going to teach. Guess what? No one showed up.

Do you know that being at a skating rink in the winter time with no heat is like being in a meat factory? And I froze. So I said, "Okay. God sent me there. I'm going. There are going to be results." My wife said, "Go ahead." I went there with one adult volunteer and two 14-year-old kids from my old church. The kids said, "We're not going to let you go there by yourself. We're going to come and watch your back." Fourteen years of age. A belief system.

One month went by and nobody came to Sunday School. I said, "Lord, you made a mistake. I'm going back to church. I can do something more with my life." But I stayed another month. Two months went by. No one showed up. I kept going on Fridays and hanging out. Kids would be fighting and I would be breaking up fights. I'm 41 years of age and it's tough.

The third and fourth months went by. No one showed up. Me, my Bible, wilting volunteers, and two teenagers who said, "We're not coming here any more."

About the fifth month, two kids showed up. Two. The rink owner's children. I'll take what I can get. Then it went to four. Then five. Then no one. Then 15 and no one. Then 15, 16, 17, 18, 19, 20, 21, 22, and then no one. And over the past three months there's been a consistent 30 and now we're up to 40. And the past three to four weeks, we finally have been able to go from having 40 kids listening to one person to having four separate classes and they're coming out.

Every Friday night when I would go to Chez Vous, my wife would say to me, "Go ahead." But after I left, she would go to bed. And one day I finally decided to ask her why she did that. She said, "I've been married to you three years. I'm going to bed because I am depressed. I don't think you're coming back." You don't know the impact of something like that.

A belief system, high-risk young people, trying to teach them that there's a life, teach them that they can cross over, teach them that they can make it, believing in them even when they hurt you.

Last week, my wife taught a seminar for all of our volunteer staff members who work with the kids. My wife has been teaching a Sunday school class for the past three weeks. My wife and I and our two-year-old son skate on Saturday nights at Chez Vous. My wife is alongside me.

And last week, God sent me a white guy from Lindenhurst, Illinois. I was praying and asking for help. I really was. God sent me this dude who came the first Friday night. We were walking the streets. I was showing him around. Three or four teenagers drove by in a car. I saw them. You know what I did? I ducked. You know why? I thought it was going to be a drive-by. It was a drive-by but not with guns. It was with mouths. They said, "Whitey, get out of here." That was Brett's first introduction to our ministry.

Today, Brett is driving the van. When it's time to leave on Friday nights, I want to go. Brett wants to hang around. So God sent me this blue-eyed white guy who has impact. Why does he have impact? Not because he's white but because he has the belief system. He loves kids and he's communicating it.

Two Friday nights ago I was at the skating rink. I was tired. So I met Brett at the skating rink. I wanted to make sure he was okay. I don't like to leave him there by himself. If something happens to him, it will make the front page of the paper because the media is watching what we're doing. I said, "Brett, hang in there. Hey man, call it a night." The kids skate from 8 to 11 p.m. and they dance from 11 to midnight. They take their skates off and they dance. And from midnight to 1:30 a.m., we're in the streets trying to help break up the gangs and get them home.

That night, I sensed something was wrong. And I stayed. There were 300 kids; too many kids. The owner made a mistake. She let in five gang members. They were in the corners and they were pumping up. You could feel it. You feel it.

Orchard Park and the Corbet Street Gang went to war. I've only been involved in one war at the skating rink. But this war was different. I prayed and asked God to stop these kids from killing each other. And I jumped into it because I felt divinely protected. I tried to separate these oxen because they grow them big now. One kid grabbed me and just threw me against the wall, and I was beat like my mama had never beat me before. Then I finally got myself together, leaned on the end of the pool table, prayed, and asked God to stop this thing. I said, "Bruce, you're 41 years of age. You're excited. Calm down. You could have a heart attack." Then the police came in and they didn't know the staff from the kids. Some of the staff members were mistakenly beaten by the police.

After it was all over, I said, "Where's Brett? Where's the white dude from Lindenhurst, Illinois, who has a belief system?" When I found him, I said, "Brett, let's get out of here." We spent an hour on the street trying to get these kids on buses, trying to separate the police from the kids. I walked to the van that was given to me by a Christian automobile dealership, opened the door, and there were 24 kids in my van. Three-quarters of the kids were from the Sunday school class. And the other kids were their friends. I said, "What are you folks doing in the van? Get out of here. I'm tired of all of you." They said, "Blame Brett. Brett told us to come to the van for safety and protection." That's where they were. And you know, driving them home, I wasn't hurting. But I was angry and I was wondering why I was doing this?

But I got to talk to all these kids who don't come to Sunday school. And our Sunday school is growing.

I've been involved in youth outreach ministry for 25 years. I talk about a lot of failures but I learned from every failure. Eighty percent of my kids at church went on to college. And some went to graduate school.

How do we teach high-risk young people? How do we reach them? With a whole lot of love. With a belief system that you need to have yourself. And with a lot of patience and a lot of time.

> *The REV. BRUCE WALL is the First Assistant Clerk Magistrate of the Boston Juvenile Court and the co-pastor of The Dorchester Temple Baptist Church in the Dorchester section of Boston.*
>
> *Rev. Wall worked for 15 years in the Twelfth Baptist Church, the Boston church home for Dr. Martin Luther King Jr.*
>
> *In 1988, Rev. Wall went to the Chez Vous Rollerway, a skating rink located in the heart of Boston's black community, and asked if he could teach a Sunday school class to teens, including gang members. In 1991, after watching his work with the youth grow, he planted a Christian church on the skating rink floor and continued his outreach ministry with young people. A year later, he moved his ministry across the street to the neighborhood police station because the heating equipment in the roller rink wasn't adequate to keep his young parishioners and their families warm on Sunday mornings.*
>
> *His essay in this volume was first presented at the 1991 symposium, "Facilitating Spiritual Growth Among At-Risk Youth."*

CHAPTER ELEVEN

Characteristics of Conversion

REV. BUSTER SOARIES

*S*ome organizations and individuals in youth care suggest that there is a group of young people in America that we can define as "at risk." And that these young people have certain characteristics. And that there is a certain methodology that can be adapted and a certain body of data that can be used in addressing the needs of these at-risk youth.

I disagree.

Between 1984 and 1989, I stood before a million kids. I looked at their faces and heard their stories. About 800,000 were middle-class white kids. About 200,000 were black kids and others. And I guess my belief today is that all kids are at risk. Further, when we consider nurturing spirituality, the nation is at risk.

And now that we've seen an absolute demise of the "evil empire" as we knew it, we're coming to understand that the evil is in us. Now that we no longer have this Russian myth looming behind our backs, we're beginning to take more seriously the notions of racism and sexism, of greed, of deception, of exploitation, of immorality and sin.

The whole nation is at risk. Half the people who get married don't stay married. Then 60 percent of those who get remarried don't stay married. I've looked at college students who have received word from their parents that they simply waited for the kids to go to college to get their divorce. So the brightest minds in our nation are having to wrestle with going back home for the first time to either mommy or daddy. It's affecting their lives. It's affecting their studies. They've never been to jail. They don't hang out on street corners. They're not members of gangs. But they're at risk.

Which makes what you do even more important than perhaps the media would suggest. For you are not marginal people who could not be successful in the real world and, therefore, settled for working with bad kids. You are the people who are developing the new models for saving this country. And we are in a mess. Thus, when I talk about young people, I talk about young people as a class. So black kids and white kids are more alike today than they've ever been before. And rich kids and poor kids are more alike today than they've ever been before.

To talk about the future of America is to talk about kids. If more of our policymakers would understand the implications for today's youth, relative to their policies, then perhaps we'd have better legislators.

To talk about the future of the church is to talk about kids. We may enjoy literature that suggests an approach to developing "be happy" attitudes. But to talk about the future of the church is to talk about kids. I've been at my assignment for the last 15 months, pastor of a Baptist church in central New Jersey — kind of a suburban, urban environment. We've had 600 people join the church in 15 months. None of them over 50. Old folks don't join churches. They stay where they are. We've had some folks leave our church. None of them over 50. The folks over 50 in our church are going to stay there, unless some circumstances dictate otherwise. The folks who join our church are young people — young parents and young people. To talk about the future of our church is to talk about young people.

To talk about the future of the American economy, is to talk about young people. To talk about the future of anything, is to talk about kids. And to think that working with youth on any level is a kind of second-class calling — work people do because they couldn't enter into the mainstream — is to suggest that you are really second-class professionals. That's how you're treated. That's how you're perceived. It goes not only with the at-risk crowd, but even in education. We have a cultural morass that requires a prophetic voice. You'll never make the cover of Wheaties for what you do. Yet, some ignorant, illiterate, irreverent athlete, paid more money in a year than you can make in a lifetime, will be on the cover of a cereal box that says, "Eat your Wheaties and be like this."

It's a cultural choice that's been made to glorify ignorance and mediocrity and frivolity, and to treat significant, important people like they don't exist. So you've got to raise money, beg rich people, convince boards of directors who say their hearts are in the right places, in addition to the work to which you've been called. It's a sad day in America when a football player can be paid a million dollars just to leave town, and you have to put kids out on corners with cans to beg for money just to buy pizza.

It's a nation at risk.

I often describe it, when I think about young people, as something that can be understood when we consider the nature of visitors, victims, and vampires.

In one sense, this generation represents something similar to visitors. I go to churches and ask them what is it they'd like me to talk to their adults about and they say, "Tell us how we can get our kids to come to church."

I pose this situation to them:

I've got a friend who works with kids from Russia who come to America on exchanges. They don't speak English. They don't know anything about our country. It's a cold turkey-type cultural visit. My friend asked me to perhaps set up a visit to a black church for them on a Sunday morning. They've never been to a black church. They don't know anything about our music or our language.

Then I say to the church members: "And what I'd like you to do is prepare for them to come to your church next Sunday. How would you prepare for them?"

The church people are quite articulate. Their ideas flow freely — everything from having a reception on the way in, to having reserved seats, to printing the bulletin in their language, to warning the congregation that these visitors are coming. In other words, that church had no difficulty anticipating their arrival and making provisions so the experience will be intact.

At the end of that exercise, then, I give them their answer: "The reason your children don't come to church is because you don't do that for them." And we don't do it for them because we fail to recognize the fact that this generation is growing up in a cultural and political and technological climate that we know not of.

In my book, *The First Chapter*, I'm arguing with kids to be a little patient with their parents because their parents know not of the world in which they live. When I was in high school, I would go horseback riding with my uncle at a place called the Triple O Ranch, about 10 miles from my hometown. The Triple O Ranch is now a shopping mall. There's a big difference between going horseback riding at Triple O Ranch with your uncle and having the next generation right behind me going to that same piece of property, and having video games and 165 stores and girls and police. It's a whole different social climate and, in some ways, I am unqualified to even project what's normal to a child who knows nothing about Triple O Ranch and everything about that shopping mall.

And to take my value system, my mores, my taboos and impose them on that child without translations or interpretation at all is to commit a gross injustice. Most of us who were born before 1955 are living on AM in a world that's on FM. You know that much of the failure that you respond to is based on the fact that there is no place for these kids to fit. So in many ways, they're visitors. Children go to school as visitors and the schools say: "Conform to what we are and, by the way, what we are is what we've always been; and if you don't, then we'll label you and kick you out."

Churches say: "Conform to what we are and what we are is very close to what we've always been; and if you don't fit in, then there's no place for you."

Society says: "Conform to what we are, and if you don't conform, then we'll reject you." Then that child has got to find his or her way to you, to make some sense out of this cultural, historical, political confusion. And you spend the rest of your life helping that child find what happened.

In many ways, we have born every day another crop of visitors who in their own country, on their own soil, are as different from everything that we consider normal as children from a foreign country. And then, worse than that, they become victims because we have a class of people who make decisions that affect the lives of these children, and those decisions more often than not invite these young people into self-destructive behavior. And then the same class of people indicts the kids for their self-destruction.

I'll give you an example. The record companies, run by a class of people we can modestly call adults, give children hundreds of thousands of dollars to make music. The music is about sexual violence. The music is about racial violence. The music breeds a whole culture of self-destruction and disrespect. And then that same class, which we can modestly call adults, indicts the children for liking the music.

Where does the music come from? From the adults. They plaster it on MTV. They glorify the people who perpetrate the music. And then we accuse the children of being the criminals. Worse than that, we crusade against drug use and ride past liquor stores and taverns and salute. Thus, the moral inconsistencies of our generation become the primary tools of victimization of this next generation. So Larry Hagman can be paid more than any other actor in Hollywood and his TV character's primary attributes are cutting dirty deals and cheating on his wife. Then a million teenage girls get pregnant, and we call them immoral.

There's something quite tragic about a class of adults who expose children to messages and models of self-destruction, and then punish the children as though they are the criminals when, in fact, they are the victims.

In light of all that, it's time to discuss conversion. Because as people of faith and as people who have gathered in an institution that's built on faith, there's got to be another dimension to our discussion that goes beyond statistics and paradigms.

When I was serving as a pastor of a little church in Harlem in 1983, I went to a high school in Patterson, New Jersey, to give a speech. It was the worst high school arguably I'd ever seen in my life. The principal took me to the bathroom and boys were smoking marijuana, and when the principal showed up, they offered him some. No fear of authority. No concern about being expelled. I'd never seen anything like this before anywhere in my life.

I was born in New York and I spent much of my childhood in New York. I'd been to large cities around the country. I'd worked with Jesse Jackson as national director of PUSH. But I'd never seen children like these before in my life.

And I'd watched the change from the Sixties, when I went to school, through the Seventies, into the Eighties. But the change was never as drastic as I had experienced at Patterson East Side High School in New Jersey. After working my way through a Martin Luther King speech, the school board said to me, "What can we do?"

I offered them two suggestions. First, get a principal who is a man and who is not afraid of these children. And the rest is history. The man came in. Brought a baseball bat in one hand, a bullhorn in the other. He was on the cover of *Time* magazine and is famous all over the world now. And his story was etched in history permanently by the movie, *Lean on Me*. Joe Clark went into that school and traumatized the whole neighborhood.

The second thing that happened wasn't discussed in the movie. I said, "Give us the school. Let me have your school. Give me that building for a week. Let me do what I do. I won't break the law, but just give me the building." By then, the school board was convinced that anybody who could do anything could have the building. If I could have taken it to New York, they'd have let me take it to New York.

We organized 22 preachers in town. And we got kids from all the churches in town to form a citywide choir. We got all the Christian teachers in town to come together to talk about evangelism in that school. We set up a citywide crusade. In the daytime we had motivational assemblies. And in the evenings we went in and talked about Jesus.

Fifteen hundred kids attend that school. Five hundred made personal commitments to become disciples of Christ that week. Two weeks later, we went for a follow-up workshop. Of the 500 kids, 491 showed up for follow-up. Those 22 churches were prepared structurally and programmatically to receive these children. And Joe Clark was able to clean that school up, in part because of his baseball bat, in part because of his bullhorn, but in part because the movement was so strong. We established a Youth for Christ office in the school. We had prayer meetings and Bible studies in that public school and the Lord came through there and cleaned that school up.

I know I'm right because I was there. Someone said to me, "What happened?" And the answer was: "We got there first." If Louis Farrakhan had shown up, there'd have been 500 new Muslims in Patterson that week.

And I meet children all over now — at McDonald's, on college campuses — who look at me and say, "I remember you. You're the guy that came to our school and preached." Some of them are in ministry. A few are probably in jail. But this is about conversion.

Why did we go? Because we took seriously the words of Jesus. Jesus said to Mary and Martha, "Your brother's dead? He'll live again." Martha said, "We know he'll live when the trumpet sounds at the final resurrection." And Jesus looked and said, "No, no, no. I am the resurrection and the life and he that believeth in Me, though he were dead, yet shall he live."

And if we're serious about an analysis of what's happening with young people today, we're talking about the living dead. A child who has been sexually abused by her daddy, who wants to go back home, is dead. A boxer who could make as much money as he wants to and insists on using his power to force himself on an 18-year-old child, is dead. A young man who has decided that his only option is to shave off all of his hair except down the middle and have different colored spikes coming around his head like a unicorn, who sits on Fisherman's Wharf and allows tourists to use him like a freak by having their pictures taken with him for a dollar — that young man is dead. A young man who would rather sell drugs than get a job is dead. They're living. They're breathing. They're functioning. But like Dracula, while they look alive, the fact is they are dead.

When we talk about young people and about youth work, we're not talking about getting kids off the streets. We can't be talking about simply having basketball leagues and nice activities to make it look like kids are doing all right. Unless our work goes to the core of what's happening, then our work is simply facilitating the evil that lurks among our children. The evil pulls them down to destruction. We can't simply be talking about social work. We've got to be talking about resurrection. And Jesus said it quite nicely. He said, "You know, I've been anointed to preach the Gospel to those who are down and set the captives free."

So then, what are the characteristics of real conversion? Stephen Jones and Barb Hargrove wrote a book called *Reaching Youth Today: Heirs to the Whirlwind.* It's a wonderful analysis of how this generation is, in fact, a unique generation. But one of the valid points they make in that book — anyone who has any relationship to the church or youth ministry whatsoever will understand — is that kids have a tendency to get converted over and over and over. Some people use the terminology "saved" and even some of the Baptists have begun to notice that kids get "saved" all the time. Sometimes kids get "saved" two and three times a day.

But what then becomes the characteristics of those who can say, "I once was blind but now I see"? Because there is that testimony. There are those among us who can say, "I've been snatched from darkness and now I walk in the marvelous light." As a matter of fact, if you look closely enough, you'll probably find a few testimonies around you. You weren't always what you are. And I certainly was not always what I am.

I have the unusual opportunity to minister in a community which is three minutes away from the campus that I attended as a college freshman. This church to which I was called was involved in a search for a pastor. The congregation votes on who the pastor will be. And while I had a reputation among most, there was one woman in our church who was a financial secretary and a registrar at the college that I attended when I was a freshman. She had a unique perspective of me as a young man who was now about to become the pastor of this great church. And her position was: "There is no way you're going to convince me that this man whom I know is fit to be my pastor."

What was she talking about? She was talking about an 18-year-old who had hair so long you could hardly see his face. An 18-year-old who on paper was majoring in urban studies and minoring in political science, but who, in fact, was majoring in girls and minoring in girls. She was talking about an 18-year-old who had wanted to call white people "devils," who was willing to reject the system and put gasoline around a building to burn it down to protest racism. And she said, "Never between now and eternity will that so-and-so be my pastor."

But I am her pastor and she is our financial secretary, and the church was so happy with our relationship after a year that it bought tickets and sent me and my wife on the first cruise we've ever been on. And that woman made the reservations. Something happened. My thesis is, if it could happen to me, it could happen to anybody.

What happened? I was dead. And now I'm alive. Let's look at it somewhat mechanically and see if we can fit it in to some theological and philosophical framework. The first thing we see in a conversion process is a predefined catalytic event. Now, I say predefined catalytic event because life comes with catalytic events. And by a catalytic event, I mean something that disrupts your norm. Something that stops you in your tracks. Something that grabs your attention. Something that becomes a compelling influence over all the major faculties in your being.

For Paul it was being knocked off his horse on the way to Damascus. That's a catalytic event. For the woman at the well, it was first being even addressed by a Jew and then having this man tell her everything about herself. And after a few minutes with Jesus, she was convinced that He was somebody that everybody needed to know and went back and said to the community, "Come see a man who told me everything that I've ever done."

For the children who gathered in our church last Friday night it was watching their 12-year-old friend lie in a casket. A healthy, wonderful, obedient, respectful child. Hit by a car. And death spoke to those children in a way that it had not in recent memory.

For the kids in Patterson, it was a sermon. A compelling verbal message — a proclamation — that caused them to assess who they were and their lives' chances.

For me it was the death of my father. I was the National Director of Operation PUSH, traveling all over the world and reporting to my childhood hero. Being trained by the man who was trained by the man who turned this nation upside down. And with a new suit on my back and press clippings from the floor to the ceiling, I picked up the telephone and heard my brother say, "Daddy died this morning." He went to the hospital for minor surgery. The surgeon was preceded by the anesthesiologist who gave him too much anesthesia and at 48 he was dead. It was a catalytic event.

But Jesus says that catalytic events are not necessarily formative toward conversion. For there are people who suffer tragedy and there are people who hear proclamations all the time. The catalytic event, the disruptive factor in one's life, becomes a step toward conversion when someone comes along and offers good news. That good news plus the catalytic event become the step toward conversion. And so the bad news is your son has AIDS, but the good news is that life is not all there is. The bad news is your momma and daddy are getting a divorce, but the good news is that there's a word somewhere that says God can supply all of your needs according to His riches and glory.

Job had some bad news. And so he raised a question: "If a man dies, shall he live again?" He didn't know the answer. Why, we had to wait centuries to get the answer. And Jesus came along and said a profound, "Yes."

And John, writing to the church in the midst of persecution, said, "I know things are tough, but beloved now we are the children of God. It does not yet appear what we shall be, but in the meantime, we're God's children right now." And the psalmist sought to capture all of that by summarizing our personhood in describing us as having been made a little lower than the angels and crowned with glory and with honor. What we attempt to do when we foster conversion is to attach good news to the catalytic events that occur in people's lives so that hopefully they'll hold on to the good news and move toward not what they are but what they can be.

So something happened. I wish I could have access to the analysis of the mind of a caterpillar. I can't find it. Nowhere can I find an analysis of the psyche of a caterpillar, because what happens to cause that caterpillar to perceive the possibility of being a butterfly doesn't seem to be common knowledge. All we know is that in the scheme of being a caterpillar, one day that caterpillar ends up going somewhere that results in its being a butterfly. Maybe the caterpillar sees the butterfly and there's caterpillar communication between the caterpillar and the butterfly. We don't know. Maybe there's a caterpillar library that caterpillars go to and read books. We don't know.

All we know is that there is something inherent in being a caterpillar that provokes caterpillars to do the right thing so God can transform them and they can experience their metamorphosis and they end up becoming butterflies. Likewise, we don't know what causes people to perceive themselves as having this higher calling and this great sense of possibility, but we do know that it's possible and so we keep doing what we do — helping them define their catalyst, a step to conversion.

It was quite graphic for these disciples, this motley crew that Jesus called his friends. For even after they had intellectually been exposed to who Jesus was, they still had to go down to Jerusalem and get some power. And they weren't ready for this great mission until Pentecost. Pentecost was a predefined catalytic event. Jesus said, "You've got some knowledge and you've got some experience, but you hang out in that room up there long enough, and something's going to happen. And when it happens, you will then be transformed in such a way that you'll be my witnesses in Jerusalem, Judea, and most parts of the world." So the Gospel then becomes the definition. And when the lives of people who undeniably will have catalytic events are attached to the Gospel, then someone says, "I yield. I can hold out no longer."

For some it only takes a sermon. For others it takes a tragedy. For others it takes a multiple set of relationships with people who care. But there's got to be a definition. Otherwise, you simply have statistics.

Now to go back to the caterpillar. The caterpillar does not leap from being a caterpillar to a butterfly. Sometimes I tell our church members that we should put a sign on the door saying, "Get yourself together and then come to church." Because we want people who dress properly, who smell sweet, who speak good grammar. You know, we want butterflies in church. Churches are generally not structured for the caterpillars. Churches are structured for butterflies. And often when I talk to churches about youth ministry, they'll raise a question: "How do we evaluate whether or not we're being effective? How do we know that our youth program is really doing what it should do in reaching those it should reach?"

Well, when your windows are being broken and your purses are being stolen and you've got graffiti in the bathrooms, then you're getting close to having an effective ministry. But if you've been working with young people for years and no one has ever stolen anything, you may be working with the wrong crowd. Or you're in a deep sense of denial.

But the cocoon then is that nurturing environment. That allows the transformation to be a process and not an event. And that's one of the great struggles we have with our evangelical and fundamentalist brothers. We want desperately the paradigm in John 9 where Jesus touches the eyes of the blind man and he instantly opens his eyes. But if you notice, most blind folk are not awakened in a moment. That's an aberration. Most healing does not occur instantaneously. And most conversion is not an event. It's a process, one that has to occur within the context of an environment that respects the process. If we don't have environments that respect the process, then we become, in the name of good, institutions that grow demons rather than perform exorcisms.

At the first church where I served, we were just a few miles outside of Newark, which meant it was quite accessible to the Newark community. It was somewhat of a suburban community. And I decided that since our roots as a church were in Newark, we had an obligation to minister to young people in Newark. And so I spoke at a junior high school graduation. After I was through a woman came up to me and she said, "Reverend Soaries, you've got to do something with my daughter. She's a gangster." And the woman was absolutely right. For this child had to be a gangster to survive where she lived. Girl Scouts didn't survive in that neighborhood. So she was a gangster by choice, and it made good sense.

So we began a specific outreach for that neighborhood. We bought a brand new bus for the church so we could pick up children from that neighborhood and bring them to our church.

One weekend when I was out of town, the kids from the neighborhood were at the church. I called back to the church to find out what was going on and the woman who answered the phone said, "Reverend, I just want you to know, one of your kids is in the bathroom."

I said, "There's nothing profound about a kid being in the bathroom. What are you saying really?"

"Well, we locked one of your kids up in the bathroom because we brought them downstairs to feed them, the way you told us to, and they got into a fight with each other," she said. "And one girl picked up another girl, slammed her back down on the floor, and we locked her in the bathroom."

I said, "Well how long did you plan on leaving her in there?"

She said, "We didn't know, but we're glad you called."

"Well, get her out of the bathroom and put her on the phone," I said. And this child comes to the phone and I said, "I understand you had a fight." She said, "Yes." I said, "Did you win?" She was silent.

That was more than 10 years ago. And to this day if you ask that child what moment in her life caused her to change her behavior, she'll say it was when the person whom she knew hated her fighting most was willing to ask her if she'd won the fight. It was clear to me that a child who at 14 had learned gangsterism as a lifestyle was not going to be changed by even the best church in the country in three weeks. It was possible for it to happen. But it was also likely that it would not. Therefore, my program and my ministry had to allow for the process of conversion.

I've got to be careful here because I don't want to sound like someone I'm not. If individual conversion is a process, and we must allow for that process to occur in a nurturing environment, then group conversion is an even greater process and we've got to allow for a nurturing environment for that group process to bring healing and conversion. When we look at the state of race relations in America today, one of the difficulties we have is accepting the fact that you can't undo in 20 years the level of oppression, repression, and suppression that has been perpetrated on the people for 300 years, whether those people are ethnics or women.

It then becomes the obligation of the people who have been the victims or the targets or the subjects to define the nature of the process. Otherwise, what we have is an institutional replica of churches that want people to change overnight.

I'm the vice president of the Gospel Music Association, which is a national organization that advocates Christian music around the world. Twenty-five on the board of directors — two blacks and 23 whites. Black folks have as their only natural resource in America, gospel music. And the white folks want to know why black folks are upset that white folks are making all the money off the music black folks have been singing all their lives. Then a guy at the board meeting looks at me and says, "Buster, you can't hold me responsible for all the racism that's ever occurred. That's the wrong issue."

The issue is whether or not we will collectively address institutional sins and understand the lingering effects of historic racism and the benefits that are derived by people who, although they are not guilty, are participants in receiving the benefits.

That does not absolve black people from moral consistency, spiritual growth, and family responsibility. But it does force a nation to reconsider institutional policies that create unnurturing environments so that the process of healing and reconciliation can begin.

You can't sign legislation in Washington and expect people to kiss and hug as if everything is all right. And if multiculturalism is going to be significant, if we're going to rise above the tribalism that separates us, then we've got to start by recognizing the need for process, which has a beginning, a middle, and an ending. And then it has some revisitation.

What I'm suggesting is that what you do, in fact, is important because in your own institutions — whether they're group homes, churches, parachurch organizations, wherever you are — you're fighting to maintain the integrity and the vibrancy of this cocoon. And folks don't like cocoons. As a matter of fact, people who appreciate cocoons most are the caterpillars who have no voice.

If you see a cocoon in your garden, it's an interruption. It doesn't fit into the aesthetic format. People don't like cocoons. The only folks who like cocoons are the caterpillars experiencing the transformation. So if you feel as though you're swimming upstream, it's because you're trying to deal with cocoons. If you feel as though the people who should understand don't understand, it's because you're attempting to build cocoons. Cocoons get in the way.

What you're attempting to do is to shelter and harbor this transformation process that happens between caterpillars and their creator. And that gets in the way. We don't want to stop watching our football game and our Super Bowl and our boxing match to hear about some caterpillar on its way to becoming a butterfly. Nor do we really want to hear about the one million children who run away every year, many from abusive situations. We don't really want to hear about the one million kids who try to commit suicide. We don't want to hear about these millions who drop out of schools. Or these teenagers who get pregnant, or the half a million who have abortions. We don't want to hear about that. Don't interrupt us. Save the nation. Save our schools. Save our factories. Just send us kids who can read, who can write, who can build the cars. Send us those kids, but don't interrupt us. Because cocoons get in the way.

So we want group homes, but not in our neighborhood. We want rehabilitation, but don't want to pay for it. We want wholesome people, but we don't want to invest in the process because cocoons get in the way. And my friends, that takes a special level of calling, to spend all of your life protecting caterpillars that are becoming butterflies from the people who would destroy the cocoons. That doesn't show up on your job description. Your job description says that you have a certain level of education and a certain set of responsibilities. Nowhere on your job description does it say that you've got to protect a little innocent nameless cocoon from a world that can kill it. That's why more often than not, on a weekly basis, you wonder how long you can do what you can do. If it were just your job, you could do it for the rest of your life. But you're involved in warfare, protecting people who can't protect themselves.

And finally, there's got to be a caring community to prevent that revictimization. There's got to be a context where the conversion can spread its wings and be a butterfly. A butterfly is not a butterfly until it begins to fly. And unfortunately, we have many aborted butterflies because the only crowd the butterfly has access to is the caterpillar.

We've got children in our church who are embarrassed when they get good grades. All of our children bring their report cards to church and we've discovered that it's important for us to give these children ovations for their success and ovations even for their attempts, because there's an overwhelming demon that lurks in their midst that pulls them down.

And as effective as the Boys Towns of this nation can be and as effective as your institutions are, you very well know that when we send children back to the environment that produced them, much of what happened in the cocoon gets stripped away. Conversion, therefore, is not simply patting a child on the back and giving him or her two or three Bible verses, and saying, "I'll meet you in Heaven."

Conversion, if it's taken seriously by the church, expands itself into the creation of a caring community, as described in Jerusalem where everybody had all things in common.

I often think about this thing when Jesus was resurrected. And 500 folks came out of their graves. Remember that part? Bible scholars debate that part a lot. But I don't deal with the debate as much as with the symbolism involved.

Think of this. Five hundred folks who were dead running downtown. There was no ticker tape parade for them at all. As a matter fact, if you read the story, when Jesus raised Lazarus from the dead, the Pharisees had a plot to kill Lazarus. What did Lazarus do? All Lazarus did was come back to life. And they wanted to kill Lazarus for being all right.

And my friends, the same people who criticize the prison systems for not doing rehabilitation, the same people who are cynical about your work and say, "You can't change these kids" — in the face of overwhelming evidence that something has happened to transform this person's life — these same people proceed to destroy the evidence.

As a society, without real appreciation for the causes of redemption, we punish people all of their lives for things that they did, even if it was a pathology that emerged from abuse. There are some folks who never wanted Mary Magdalene to be in the crowd because of what she had been.

A caring community suggests that there is something for that young man or that young woman when he or she leaves the cocoon, that there are intentional opportunities when he or she leaves that prison cell.

A friend of mine down at Tennessee State Prison has been working for years with a group of young men who have now formed themselves into a faith community called "Faith Ministry." They are in prison for an assortment of crimes, and none of them look like Christians. None of them look like anything much. But this minister, this prophet, who has been going in on Tuesday nights and working with these young men, formed them into a group in society. One of the things he could do is use their musical talents to help liberate them from not only where they were intellectually and spiritually, but also from where they were economically and otherwise. He's having a tough time, because the state won't accept the fact that they have changed.

Our nation is at risk when we have a theology of nonredemption as the operative theology in our culture. We have on our money, "In God We Trust," yet we don't trust in God. We don't have a theology of redemption. We don't believe people can change. And if we don't believe people can change, then we won't create structures that facilitate the maintenance of the transformation that's taken place.

Now one thing that we have in kids is this kind of faith and hope and sense of possibility. What are the characteristics of a caring community, this connection to sustaining the conversion process?

It's got to be structure that has eye-high expectations. To the extent that we are successful working with people after they have been changed would indicate that we expect something from them. I don't expect that young lady who was involved in the fight at church — she now is an officer at Citibank and a college graduate — to go to church today and slam someone on her back. I'm sure she's not forgotten how to do it, but if I expect her to do it, she'll do it.

One of the most vicious forms of racism is when white liberals deal with black, Hispanic, and other minority kids as if those kids cannot rise to a level of excellence, and accept mediocrity. High expectations mean that teachers insist on proper grammar. My boys are two years and four months old, and I discovered when they first started talking that they could respond to the question, "How are you doing?" That was the good news. The bad news was that they would say, "I'm doing good."

Two years old. My fear is that that will become a part of their psyche and a part of their normal speech pattern, and if I don't correct it, then they'll score lower on their SATs. Because you can't say, "I'm doing good" in response to the question, "How are you doing?" The word "doing" is a verb which means you need an adverb.

As I sat my boys down a few weeks ago and gave them a lecture, my wife heard me — she thought I was on the phone — and came into the TV room. She thought I had lost my mind. I said to the boys, "Now, Malcolm, all right. Sit down. It's time for us to have a man-to-man talk. Now when I ask you the question, 'How are you doing?', the answer is a description of the word 'doing.' And the word 'doing' is a verb. And the word 'good' is an adjective. You can't use that word to answer that question. You need a word like 'well.' And so I want you to use an adverb when I say, 'How are you doing?' You say, 'I'm doing well.'"

They may not know the grammar, but you call my house right now, and they'll say, "I'm doing well." They may be black. They may not have as much money as the Rockefellers and the Kennedys. But they're going to be able to say, "I'm doing well" because I have high expectations for my boys. And my family will be a nurturing environment and will be a caring community, if I have high expectations.

Absolution also is important. It's got to be possible for a person to be forgiven of his or her sins and have the slate wiped clean. Because if we can't, then none of us is qualified to do what we do. We've got to come with a theology of absolute forgiveness of sins. Though your sins be of scarlet, they can be as white as snow. If we confess our sins, God is faithful to forgive us of our sins and cleanse us of all unrighteousness. We have got to believe that baptism means the death of the old and the resurrection of the new, that a caring community never reminds a person of where they came from.

A caring community involves not only a teacher, but also a coach. Have you ever noticed that a coach can get away with anything? A coach can cuss. A coach can use his or her hands. When I was in school, teachers couldn't beat you but the coach could kick your butt. We need more coaches — people who are engaged and involved and are never satisfied with anything less than a victory.

And then we need consequences. For even after conversion, people will make mistakes. And young people have got to know, that while we love them, there are consequences for their behavior. We have to have the kind of standards that remind them that while we forgive them and accept the fact that they've changed, that none of us is perfect. All of us sin. And there are consequences attached to our behavior.

Which is why, when we talk about "safe sex," we've got to start with abstinence. Because if we don't start with abstinence, then safe sex is linked only to pregnancy. But what about the girl in my high school who never got pregnant but whose reputation was so ruined that she had to leave town to find a husband?

What about the eternal consequences? The Kingdom consequences of people who violate the sanctity of their bodies. Sex cannot simply be summarized by those who get pregnant and those who don't. But there are consequences attached to all of our actions. We invest in what we become by what we do today. And a caring community brings all of those factors to bear.

When we talk about conversion we're talking about, in my estimation, a predefined catalytic event, a nurturing environment which is an incubator, like a cocoon. And a caring community which makes lifelong connection and provides social and spiritual alternatives for the converted.

I suggest that there should be nothing that can stop us from doing this noble work. When I consider the extent to which we may have to go, I think about the man who was at the bottom of a ditch. And his friend came along with a rope to pull him out. But the rope was too short. And the man said, "I'll be right back." And he got a second rope. The second rope was a little longer, but he still couldn't reach his friend. Then he said, "I'll be right back." And he got a third rope. And the third rope was longer than the first two ropes, but it still could not reach his friend. And the man said, "I've done all I can do." He had lost hope. But his friend had not been in the ditch so long he had lost his mind. So he called his friend from the bottom of the ditch and said, "Get the ropes and tie them together. Get me out of here."